Rural Dacia: The Untold Story

Eloise Smart

Table of Contents

ABSTRACT..5

CHAPTER 1 Introduction...6

    1.1 Introduction to Dacia..7
    1.2 The Iron Age Dacians before Rome..9
    1.3 Dacia's Interactions with Rome...13
    1.4 Introduction to Sarmizegetusa...18

CHAPTER 2 Establishing the Colony..24

    2.1 Romanization in the Provinces..24
    2.2 Successful Romanization in Gaul..28
    2.3 Trajan's Dacian Campaigns...31
    2.4 City Planning in 106 CE..36

CHAPTER 3 A Roman City in Dacia...41

    3.1 City Engineering...41
    3.2 A Local Production Center..50
    3.3 Roman Depictions of Dacians...61

CHAPTER 4 Identity at Sarmizegetusa..65

    4.1 Becoming Roman?..65
    4.2 The Big Picture...74
    4.3 A New Perspective..75

CHAPTER 5 Conclusions...79

    5.1 A Changed Landscape..79
    5.2 Going Forward..80

FIGURES..82

Abstract

In recent years, archaeologists have proven that Roman provinces such as Gaul successfully underwent the process of Romanization, or the process by which Roman and native cultures blended to create a new provincial cultural identity and where the archaeological evidence showed that native populations culturally assimilated to Roman life. Likewise, Romans accepted local populations into Roman life and oftentimes syncretized aspects of their own culture with that of the locals. This process was usually stimulated by the creation of Roman cities and colonies throughout the province from which Roman culture emanated. However, Dacia's capital city, Colonia Ulpia Traiana Augusta Dacica Sarmizegetusa, which was founded in 106 CE under Trajan after the Second Dacian War (105-6 CE), doesn't exhibit these qualities of Romanization. The colony was set up for Trajan's Legio IV Flavia Felix legionary veterans from the Dacian Wars. The material culture, including architecture, ceramics, inscriptions on stelae, and other artifacts, expresses a purely Roman aesthetic in terms of style and construction. The evidence suggests that native Dacians were not successfully Romanized, either because of a conscious rejection of Roman life or a refusal by the Romans to successfully incorporate the locals into the new Roman province. Due to the violence of the two Dacian Wars and the speed with which Rome begins to colonize the province, I suggest that both scenarios are possible for why Romanization failed in Dacia and if Romanization did occur, it didn't emanate from the capital city but from rural settlements closer to the *limes*, many of which have not yet been excavated extensively.

Chapter 1: Introduction

Acquired under Trajan in 106 CE and abandoned under Aurelian between 271 and 275 CE, Dacia is a unique province because of its brief Roman occupation and the enigmatic relationship the Romans shared with the newly conquered natives. The early withdrawal of Roman administration after only 169 years makes this study especially relevant to Roman provincial studies today. In early studies of the provinces, scholars emphasized the ways in which the Romans dominated and "civilized" the peoples they conquered. The Romanization of a province was studied by looking only for evidence of Roman material culture and constructions, with little emphasis on the native population, material evidence of their presence, and how they received Roman culture. Recent publications about the provinces have attempted to correct this bias towards a Romano-centric view of cultural identity and exchange.[1]

In order to study this process in Dacia, Ulpia Traiana Augusta Dacica Sarmizegetusa can be analyzed for evidence of Roman and native material culture including architectural, ceramic, and epigraphic remains. The city was founded as a Roman veteran colony for Legio IV Flavia Felix, which makes the heavy Roman military and civilian presence unremarkable. However, there is a conspicuous lack of Dacian material culture at Dacia's new capital, suggesting that the relationship between the Romans and natives was fractious. Provinces such as Gaul have shown that one avenue of Romanization was the establishment of Roman cities at strategic locations throughout a province, from which Roman culture could permeate into the local landscape, creating economic, social,

---

[1] Mattingly 2004, 5-6 and Woolf 2000, 123.

and religious ties with the local populations. I argue that this model is inverted in Dacia, with the Roman city acting instead as a hindrance to cultural exchange.

Introduction to Dacia

The province of Dacia is located in the modern state of Romania, though some of its borders extended into neighboring states (Figure 1).[2] The geography of the region has been described as consisting of mountains, hills, and plains, with a number of meandering rivers throughout these features that allow for an ease of travel.[3] The Carpathian mountains, some of which rise to a height of 2500 meters, create a natural barrier around the low-lying hills and alluvial plains, and this bowl in the center of the mountains is most often referred to as Transylvania.[4] Transylvania makes up the heartland of both ancient Dacian and modern Romania, and the landscape today is dominated mostly by forest interspersed with agricultural land. The Carpathian Mountains were formed in the Meso-Cretaceous period (145-66 million years ago) and are rich in metal ores such as gold and silver, hence the name Metalliferi Mountains for the Western Carpathians. In fact, it has been estimated that some 1.3 tons of gold were extracted in the 169 years of Roman occupation from these mountains.[5]

Transylvania is known for less precious but similarly attractive resources, such as iron and salt, which were exploited from prehistoric times. Iron metallurgical technology was transmitted from the Celts to the Dacians, but iron was most readily exploited by the

---

[2] Parts of Hungary, Bulgaria, Poland, Moldova, Serbia, Ukraine, and Slovakia are also included in Dacia's overall extent.
[3] Haynes and Hanson 2004, 12.
[4] Transylvania, comes from the Latin "trans silvae" or "beyond the forests".
[5] Otlean 2007, 39.

Romans, along with large salt deposits throughout the region.[6] Gold, silver, iron, and salt are all precious commodities and evidence of their exploitation has been traced to both the Dacians and the Romans. Besides these natural resources and the general topography of the area, the climate was also desirable for ancient settlement.

The climate of the area is consistent with the rest of Eastern Europe, being described as temperate-continental.[7] Summers are hot and winters cold, with abundant marshlands and consistent rainfall that yields rich soil for agriculture. There is evidence that early Dacians built upon steeply terraced hillsides to exploit this rich soil, and faunal evidence from Dacian citadels suggests that cereals were the staple of Dacian diets.[8] Though the ancient climate of Dacia can't be exactly reconstructed, evidence of vine cultivation and agricultural patterns suggest that ancient Dacia had a similar climate to Romania today.

Multiple altitudinal zones throughout the area provide a wide range of flora and fauna that were exploited by the ancient inhabitants. Cereal cultivation and animal husbandry were staples of pre-Roman Dacia, and both of these forms of domestication increased under Roman rule.[9] It is generally accepted that a governmental policy of deforestation during the Industrial Age has altered the overall landscape of Romania, especially the lowlands, where agriculture is most prolific. Ioana Otlean argues that wood would have been more abundant in pre-Roman and Roman periods even within these lowlands, since most Dacian and Roman constructions and tools were made of wood.[10] Thus the general topography, natural resources, and overall climate of Dacia provide a rich and

---

[6] Ibid., 39.
[7] Ibid., 31.
[8] Haynes and Hanson 2004, 14.
[9] Otlean 2007, 35-6.
[10] Ibid., 38.

diverse environment for early human settlement, and demonstrate that Dacia was a naturally attractive bounty for the ever-expanding Roman Empire.

The Iron Age Dacians before Rome

Before the Romans invaded Dacia, the area had already enjoyed a long history of occupation. The fertile lands of Transylvania show human occupation from the Neolithic, and the Bronze Age in Dacia is well attested with a shift from stone to metal tools along with faunal and floral cultivation. It was with the introduction of iron metallurgy in the region that the Geto-Dacian cultures north of the Danube emerged, collectively known as the La Tène Iron Age. This period in Romanian history is referred to as the La Tène culture, which gave birth to the many related tribes north of the Danube. This group of people can be assessed in the archaeological record by their settlement patterns, pottery traditions, burials, and coinage.[11]

The Dacians had several kinds of settlements including open settlements like farms or villages, defended settlements in naturally defendable upland terraces, dispersed settlements in mountainous regions, and nucleated settlements in mountainous regions built on natural or artificial terraces.[12] Undefended settlements are the most commonly identified type, but the least excavated. Dacian buildings in these sorts of settlements are semi-sunken, usually 3 to 4 meters across and 4 to 5 meters long with a depth of 70 to 80 cm. Some pits have been excavated which are inverted-funnel shaped and were probably grain storage pits. Most of the excavated sites of this type are low-density agricultural

---

[11] The Dacian pottery assemblage will be addressed in chapter 3.
[12] Lockyear 2004, 36. After Glodariu's *Arhitectura Dacilor* 1985.

settlements, which were largely unaffected by large-scale political change.[13] Defended settlements are of two types, those with *murus dacicus* (defensive walls made of large cut stones with no mortar between the blocks) and those without. Those without these walls usually had earthen-covered wooden fortifications along with ditches. These settlements could be called 'promontory forts", since they are situated in strategically defensible positions on hilltops.[14]

The defended citadels with *murus dacicus* were those of the type that Decebalus' capital, Sarmizegetusa Regia, belongs to. Using Sarmizegetusa Regia as a template, these sites have a large defensive wall made up of characteristic blocks around a fortified area. There is a ceremonial site, domestic homes, and workshops located outside of the fortified center (Figure 2).[15] The domestic settlements are scattered in the woods across several terraces near the fortress. The buildings in these settlements are all timber with stone foundations or with post-holes. They were made of waddle-and-daub walls and were both circular and rectangular in shape. At Sarmizegetusa Regia, one building was 20 sided and had a diameter of 12.5 meters. Inside this structure was found a conical vessel with the words "Decebalus per Scorilo" stamped on it in four places, another clue that this site is associated with Decebalus.[16] Workshops identified at the site are mostly for iron working and two separate circular sanctuaries have been identified.

Circular and rectangular sanctuaries or temples have been identified at several Dacian sites, though the most well-excavated are at Sarmizegetusa Regia. There is no

---

[13] Ibid., 40.
[14] Ibid., 41.
[15] Ibid., 43. This site is thought to be Decebalus' capital because of the Roman military presence attested around the entire site. A Roman bath has been found as well as multiple Latin inscriptions and Roman military items. It is likely that Romans occupied the hillfort after partly destroying it, though it is not clear when they abandoned the site.
[16] Ibid., 44.

catalogue of finds associated with the large sanctuaries at Sarmizegetusa Regia, though one sanctuary at a site called Piatra Craivii had a ritual pit with animal bones and pottery fragments inside it.[17] These sanctuaries are even more perplexing since none can be attached to a particular religious function or worship of a god. The main Dacian deity, Zalmoxis, is not represented ichnographically by the Dacians, nor is he associated with any particular ritual architecture.[18] The mystery cult of Zalmoxis was introduced in Dacia in the early 5th century BCE and centers on the concept of a life after death, represented by Zalmoxis returning from the underworld after three years.[19] Though Zalmoxis is not depicted, the lack of Dacian religious imagery is not total. There are some metal objects such as a helmet from Coțofenești from the 4th century BCE that depicts riders on horseback on one cheek guard and a warrior kneeling over a bound sacrificial ram on the other.[20] These images have been interpreted as religious, since it is believed that feasting was an important aspect of Dacian religion. Another example of religious feasting is a Dacian *rhyton* from the 3rd century BCE found at Poroina (Figure 3). This libation vessel is in the shape of a ram and four women hold ram *rhyta* aloft on the neck, suggesting the way this item would be used in ritual.[21]

Dacian burials from the Iron Age vary. A hilltop at Cugir has a necropolis with several *tumuli*. One cremation burial here consisted of a body placed on a cart with three sacrificed horses and then burnt. The remains were then covered in clay and then covered with an imported Italian bronze *situla* and a pedestal bowl. Burnt fragments of the cart, weapons, armor, silver decorations and a gold plaque were found and the burial is dated

---

[17] Ibid., 62.
[18] Ibarra 2014, 171.
[19] Ibid.
[20] Ibid., 173.
[21] Ibid.

to the first half of the 1st century BCE.[22] This type of burial seems to be an exception, and since only about 300 individuals from Romania have been excavated spread over four centuries, it is difficult to make sweeping assumptions about Dacian burial practices or beliefs about death.[23]

Lastly, the Dacians had a coinage system from the 3rd century BCE, probably influenced by the Black Sea Greek city-states monetary system. Production of local coins in Dacia had relatively small distributions, though each new issue of coin types increased in quantity and circulation.[24] However, Roman Republican *denarii* are found in a disproportionate number throughout Transylvania, both in single circulation and in a surprising number of hoards. There is also evidence of high-quality copies, some so good that they are hard to identify. The first influx of these *denarii* seems to be between 75 and 65 BCE with a smaller influx during the 40's and 30's BCE.[25] Copying might have begun after the Romans curtailed the influx in 65 BCE and continued down to the Dacian Wars.

The wider questions about why Dacians wanted these *denarii* and what was happening in Rome and Dacia that facilitated this large influx are not within the scope of this paper. The coin evidence does, however, add to the overall picture of Dacian life before the Roman conquest. Kris Lockyear argues that the diverse settlement patterns, the lack of uniformity in burial practices, the increased use of coinage, and the low-density of pottery all suggest that there was a distinct period of regional diversity. Lockyear sees the presence of the *denarii* and the amount of copying not as evidence of increased trade but as increased competition and power politics between smaller factions. This interpretation

---

[22] Lockyear 2004, 63-4.
[23] Ibid., 65.
[24] Ibid.
[25] Ibid.

also explains the low population densities in most Dacian settlements and the increased number of fortified settlements. Furthermore, the sanctuaries at Sarmizegetusa Regia could have represented a sacred place for a wider community and the scattered domestic settlements on the terraces could be reinterpreted not as family groups but as competing elite residences.[26] This sort of competition among Dacian elites in the 2nd century CE may be another facet of the story of Roman and Dacian interactions that led up to the Dacian Wars.

Dacia's Interactions with Rome

The Romans had a general rather than specific understanding of Dacian land and customs. The ancient authors attempted to make the distinction between the Getae and the Dacians, with Herodotus saying,

"οἱ δὲ Γέται πρὸς ἀγνωμοσύνην τραπόμενοι αὐτίκα ἐδουλώθησαν,

Θρηίκων ἐόντες ἀνδρηιότατοι καὶ δικαιότατοι."

"But the Getae, being the best and most just of the Thracians, having turned towards arrogance, were enslaved."[27]

Strabo also attempted to elucidate the distinction between these two groups of people:

"γέγονε δὲ καὶ ἄλλος τῆς χώρας μερισμὸς συμμένωνἐκ παλαιοῦ· τοὺς μὲν γὰρ Δακοὺς προσαγορεύουσιτοὺς δὲ Γέτας, Γέτας μὲν τοὺς πρὸς τὸν Πόντ ονκεκλιμένους καὶ πρὸς τὴν ἕω, Δακοὺς δὲ τοὺς εἰς. τἀναντία πρὸς τὴν Γε ρμανίαν καὶ τὰς τοῦἼστρου πηγάς..."

---

[26] Ibid., 70.
[27] Herodotus, *Histories* Volume 1, 4.93.1. All translations presented in this paper are my own.

> "But there is another division of the place kept in place from older times: for some are called Dacian and others called Getae. The Getae are those who lean towards the Pontus and the dawn (East), the Dacian, those who lean towards the opposite direction (West), Germany and the waters of the Ister(Danube)..."[28]

Strabo's positioning of the Dacians and the Getae is surprisingly accurate, most likely because of the trade between the Dacians and the Greek city-states along the coast of the Black Sea.[29] It is important, however, to keep in mind that all literary records that describe the Dacians are written from the biased position of Romans and Greeks who viewed these people as uncivilized barbarians.

The many tribes that made up the Dacian people were first united into one nation under King Burebista in the 1st century BCE. Few records of this man are extant, but Strabo mentions that he was a Getan who was able to unite his own tribe before conquering his neighbors and establishing a "μεγάλην ἀρχὴν" or a "great empire".[30] The extent of this "empire" has been disputed by modern scholars, some of whom don't believe that a true state was formed, but rather a loose confederacy of domains under his rule.[31] Whatever the extent of his power, Burebista was assassinated and a succession of less powerful kings ruled polities within Dacia while establishing a formidable reputation among the Romans. The first centuries BCE and CE were fraught with tales of Dacian military

---

[28] Strabo, *Geography*, 7.3.12.
[29] Strabo himself was from Turkey, only 75 km from the Black Sea.
[30] Strabo, *Geography*, 7.3.11.
[31] Lockyear 2004, 69. Lockyear sees the diversity within Late Iron Age Dacian pottery assemblages, settlement constructions, burial practices, and sanctuaries as evidence that there was no overarching religious, ethnic, or political apparatus that united these tribes into an "empire" or "state".

threats and Dacian raids across the Danube on Roman land.[32] It is clear that the increased prosperity and military power of the Geto-Dacian people was bolstered by trade and interaction with the Roman world, but political centralization and military fortifications throughout Dacia were also consequences of these interactions with Rome.[33] Whether or not the threats of Dacian raids and military incursions were accurate, the Romans clearly saw the Dacians as a rising military power in the region that threatened the security of the Roman Empire even as early as the Augustan Age.

These fears came to fruition with Domitian's Dacian War in 87 CE. The Dacians and Romans had a tenuous relationship of reciprocity in place that created a clientship relationship of Roman subsidies paid to Dacian kings. Driven by the constant need to fund his numerous armies, Domitian refused to pay these subsidies any longer, at which point the Dacians reestablished their raids south of the Danube.[34] The fragile relationship between the two states soured, and Domitian sent troops into Dacia, which by this time was ruled by King Decebalus, the last of Dacia's kings.[35] Sending the Romans multiple messages suing for peace but requesting outlandish sums of money, Decebalus lured the Romans, led by Cornelius Fuscus, from the safety of their camps and supply lines deep into Dacian territory and ambushed them, decimating the legion and killing C. Fuscus himself.[36] A second campaign in 88 under Tettius Julianus was much more successful for Rome, with the Romans penetrating as far as Decebalus' hillfort capital, Sarmizegetusa Regia, and Decebalus suing for peace again. Success seemed imminent for Domitian, but

---

[32] Dio Cassius, *Roman History*, 51.22.8. Dio Cassius explains how the Dacians switched sides from Octavian to Antony prior to Actium, though he claims they gave Antony little help.
[33] Musat and Ardeleanu 1985, 41.
[34] Ibid., 40.
[35] Dio Cassius, *Roman History*, 67.6.1.
[36] Musat and Ardeleanu 1985, 42.

war on the German border in 89 made further war with Dacia inadvisable and a temporary peace was reached.[37]

Domitian's disastrous campaign of 88 set the stage for Trajan's robust war efforts in 101-2 and 105-6 CE. Dio Cassius notes that Trajan gathered 100,000-150,000 men, around 22% of the entire Roman army, to wage his wars. This time, Decebalus was less successful both in his diplomacy and his war efforts. Trajan had learned from the painful defeat of C. Fuscus, and had carefully planned the route of the troops and their supply lines through the mountain passes to Decebalus' stronghold at Sarmizegetusa Regia. The campaigns were successful, and Trajan's troops razed Decebalus' capital to the ground after Decebalus himself committed suicide to escape dishonor. As the artists of Trajan's column in Rome depict, Trajan's men systematically built bridges, improved roads, and established camps as they steadily advanced through Dacian countryside, skirmishing with Dacian forces along the way. The infrastructure laid by these military engineers in the initial war of 101-2 proved helpful not only in the second campaign from 105-6, but also in the establishment of the Roman province in 106. Settlers were able to easily follow these new routes into Dacia, which may have been a factor in how quickly the city of Sarmizegetusa was established after the cessation of hostilities.

One of the most remarkable aspects of this new settlement was its name. After defeating the Dacians and supposedly burning their capital, Trajan names his own capital of the province Sarmizegetusa after the Dacian capital. When the Romans defeated Corinth in 146 BCE, they waited 102 years before reestablishing a colony there under Julius Caesar in 44 BCE.[38] Waiting three generations allowed time for the memory of destruc-

---

[37] Dio Cassius, *Roman History*, 67.7.2.
[38] Romano 2006, 66.

tion to fade sufficiently. This meant that when the Romans began to build upon the site, animosity from the local population was minimized and the Romans rebuilt the city to their specifications. That Trajan renames his new capital after the capital of his conquered enemy not two years after the close of the Dacian Wars is significant. The use of the name Sarmizegetusa may have been Trajan's attempt at retaining a local provincial aesthetic, since he doesn't name the site after any of his legions stationed in Dacia. However, the short time period between the destruction of the old capital and the founding of the new one seems tactless at best and malicious at worst.

Introduction to Sarmizegetusa

The archaeological site of Sarmizegetusa is located in the small village of Sarmizegetusa, Hunedoara County, Romania (Figure 4). The city's full name, given by Hadrian, is *Colonia Ulpia Traiana Augusta Dacica Sarmizegetusa*.[39] The full inscription reads,

> "[Imp(erator) Ca[es(ar)] Div[i] Ne[r]v[a]e f[ilius] Nerva Trai[a]n[us] /
> [Aug(ustus) Germanicus] D[acicus, p]ontif(ex) max(imus), trib(unicia)
> pot(estate) [...i]m[p(erator) VI,] /

---

[39] Daicoviciu 2004, 92. Other inscriptions from the site make it clear that Sarmizegetusa was used in the name of the town from its inception.

[co(n)s(ul) V, p(ater) p(atriae, col(oniam) Ulpiam Trai]ana[m Augusta]m Dacic(am) [Sar]miz[egetusam fecit]

OR

[co(n)s(ul) V, p(ater) p(atriae), forum col(oniae) Ulpiae Trai]anae Dacic(ae) [Sar]miz[egetusae fecit]" (Figure 5).

This name imbues several meanings upon the site. First, it was established by Trajan, whose given name, Marcus Ulpius Traianus, reflected the gens of his family. The Ulpii were a respectable family of Roman colonists living in Hispania during the first century CE. Secondly, Trajan, as Augustus, created the colony as a decree of the Roman emperor, imbuing its founding with Imperial power. Lastly, Trajan chose to keep the name Sarmizegetusa for the capital of Dacia, even though Sarmizegetusa Regia lies 40 km away in the mountains.

The site was first discovered in 1495 by Johannes Mezerzius, a priest from Alba Iulia, who recorded several visible inscriptions.[40] Some of the buildings that were above ground level were sketched by S.J. Hohenhausen, an Austrian army major, in a book published in 1775.[41] The first semi-scientific excavations were carried out by M. J. Ackner who discovered several mosaics, inscriptions, and reliefs in 1832. Romanian scholars George Cupcea and Felix Marcu note that there were sporadic excavations after 1832 and became more regular with the establishment of the Society of History and Archaeology of the Hunedoara County in 1881.[42] The establishment of the Society also brought to an end the unrestrained destruction of the site that had been undertaken through much of the 1800's. Roman bricks had been reused to build churches, marble monuments were converted into lime, and monuments and inscriptions were taken from the site to adorn cas-

---

[40] Cupcea and Marcu 2011, 543. Dorin Alicu et al. in Small Finds from a publication titled *Ulpia Traiana Sarmizegetusa* say that Johannes retrieved the inscriptions at the end of 1500 rather than 1495.
[41] Alicu, et al. 1994, 3.
[42] Cupcea and Marcu 2011, 543.

tles and private homes.[43] Following the creation of the Society, the Museum of Archaeology in Deva was created to house many of the finds from intermittent digs between 1880 and 1893.

The Committee for Historical Monuments for Transylvania began to protect and preserve the site and its objects by 1921 and official excavations began at the site in 1924 under archaeologist Constantin Daicoviciu. Between 1924 and 1937 the "palace of the Augustales", the forum, the amphitheatre, the mausoleum of the Aurelii, two suburban villas, and several necropoleis were excavated. These excavations ceased in 1938 due to the beginning of World War II.[44] Excavations were resumed in 1973 by Hadrian Daicoviciu and Ioan Piso and continued into the 1980's. During these excavations, the financial procurator's house was discovered within the walls of the main enclosure. The remains of several temples and the amphitheatre, which lay north of this enclosure, were further excavated as well. To the south and east of the main enclosure some pottery and brick workshops were found, indicating the presence of production zones within the city.[45] Another of Sarmizegetusa's key modern excavators is Alexandru Diaconsecu, who has published extensively on the Trajanic forum at the site since 1973.

The sites original main enclosure was 530 by 430 meters and covered 22.5 hectares, but was later extended to encompass 32.4 hectares. The *extra muros* extent of the city may have covered an additional 500-600 square meters and covered 100 hectares.[46] The main enclosure was designed and modeled on the Roman orthogonal military camp or the *castrum*. Other than archaeological evidence, knowledge of the Roman camp lay-

---

[43] Alicu, et al. 1994, 4.
[44] Ibid.
[45] Gazdac and Cocis 2004, 10.
[46] Otlean 2007, 165.

out comes from the *De Munitionibus Castrorum* by Hyginus Gromaticus or a pseudo-Hyginus. Some of the features included were defensive walls with four circular towers at each corner, and the *cardo maximus* and *decumanus maximus* that created the two major North-South and East-West roads respectively (Figure 6.A). Their intersection at the center of the camp is the *Principia* or the camp headquarters. The Roman *castrum* model was uniform for all military encampments across the Empire, with some modifications for local terrain always included. These military camps would often become small towns and cities as their military purpose was downgraded, and by the second century CE the design of the *castrum* was used as a model for city-buildings even when a military instillation was not the main purpose of the settlement.

These features of a military *castrum* can be seen clearly at Sarmizegetusa, though the *Principia* of a military camp was replaced by the *forum* of the ancient town. This *forum* was first identified by Constantin Daicoviciu as the "palace of the Augustales" or a priestly college (Figure 6.B). This particular interpretation of the structure is puzzling, since its location at the juncture of the *cardo maximus* and *decumanus maxiumus* in the center of the town would suggest that the structure is the *forum*. What might have perplexed Daicoviciu was the presence of a second *forum* area to the south of the main *forum* (Figure 7). Modern scholars now agree that the larger *forum* is the Forum of Trajan and the smaller *forum* to the south is a *macellum*, or covered Roman marketplace, since the original dedicatory inscription for the main *forum* has been excavated (Figure 5.C).[47] Its creation, which happened at the same time as the main *forum* was being converted from wooden construction to stone, was probably meant to expand the main *forum* and allow for a growing populace to conduct business in both public spaces.

---

[47] Diaconescu 2004, 92.

Several *insulae* have been excavated to the south of the forum and the house of the financial procurator of Dacia was identified by Daicoviciu in the northeastern section of the main enclosure. Two *horrea,* or public warehouses, were discovered adjacent. The *insulae* have been excavated since 1999 under the direction of Ioan Piso and consist of several houses with porticos framing the sides that faced the east and west *cardines*.[48] Some homes were in the Greek peristyle house tradition with the rooms centered around a courtyard, while others were corridor houses, a housing model found in Pannonia and other regions along the Danube.[49] The financial procurator's home has been identified as such because of its departure from these peristyle homes (Figure 6.D). It occupied a large part of an *insula* block in the northeast of the city and it is located next to the two *horrea,* which would have held supplies for the city and the Province at large.

The amphitheatre is located outside of the city center to the north of the main enclosure (Figure 6.E). One coin issued between 99 and 101 and three issued between 119 and 121 were found in secure deposits of the earliest wooden construction. These coins are evidence that the amphitheatre was constructed in the later years of Trajan's reign and the early years of Hadrian's. Estimates of the ancient city's population based on the size of the amphitheatre have been much contested. Early population estimates were between 10,000 and 20,000 while later excavations suggested numbers as high as 25,000 and 30,000.[50] The latter number is now generally believed to be too high, even for the later phases of the city where the main enclosure grew to 32.4 hectares. Under Antoninus Pius in 158 CE the amphitheatre was refurbished in stone and next to the amphitheatre a build-

---

[48] Ibid., 98.
[49] Ibid., 99.
[50] Alicu and Paki 1995, 9.

ing with private dwelling and *thermae* has been recognized as a possible gladiator school.[51]

An *area sacra* has been identified to the east of the amphitheatre (Figure 6.F). A temple of Nemesis, a temple of Aesculapius and Hygeia, a temple of Liber Pater, a temple of Silvanus, and a large unidentified temple have been excavated. A shrine to Mithras and an altar to the Imperial cult were also discovered. Inscriptions note that Palmyrean priests erected a temple, though it doesn't specify which temple or to whom it was dedicated.[52] The diverse number of gods worshiped in the city speaks to its cosmopolitan nature, though the absence of any cult worship of native Dacian gods is poignant.

Additionally, several pottery, glass, and iron smelting workshops have been identified. Brick, tile, and pottery kilns were identified in the southeast of the city, while a stonemason's workshop was located in the inner sanctuary of the temple of Aesculapius and Hygeia and a glass workshop was located west of the temple of Silvanus.[53] All of these architectural elements point to a robust Roman populace in the centuries following the Dacian Wars. Several public buildings one would expect to find in a Roman city, such as a Capitolium (a temple to the Capitoline triad of Jupiter, Juno, and Minerva), large public bath houses, and a theater have not been found. The architectural features of Sarmizegetusa reflect those of a provincial Roman city designed for Roman citizens. The lack of native elements at the site must now be addressed to ascertain if this lack is due to modern bias or ancient reality.

---

[51] Daicoviciu 2004, 99 and Alicu and Paki 1995, 19.
[52] Ibid., 18.
[53] Ibid., 24-5.

Chapter 2: Establishing the Colony

Romanization and the Provinces

In the past twenty years, the word "Romanization" has been criticized for its imperialistic connotations and examined for its relevance in Roman provincial literature. Some scholars prefer to do away with the word entirely. This rejection of the term has its roots in Romanization's 19th century British imperialist origins first espoused by Francis Haverfield, an Oxford trained archaeologist. Haverfield had borrowed the term from Theodor Mommsen, one of his academic advisors. His view of Romanization closely resembled what we would now call imperialism, where the colonizing nation subjugates a barbarian people while exploiting them socially, economically, and politically. Haverfield painted a rosy picture of Rome civilizing the barbarian nations and bestowing peace, urbanization, and Roman law upon them. This view of Romanization is damaging not only because it is a gross misrepresentation of the process, but it also helped justify Britain's imperialist attitude towards the disenfranchised nations under her rule, including Egypt, India, and many more.[54]

Thus the term has been closely linked with a British political program that 21st century scholars largely view negatively, and has caused wary scholars to question its usefulness as a term for understanding the complex process of Roman/native interactions. There have been several attempts to find a more suitable term. Stephen Chappell completely rejects Romanization as too "Romano-centric" and prefers to use "new cultural formation".[55] He feels that the historically politicized nature of the term Romanization in Romania makes it too contentious of a term to use. David Mattingly has further questioned the use of the term by suggesting it can only be implemented as a "top-down perspective of ancient society" and that this perspective hinders scholars from identifying anyone in the material record other than elites.[56] He prefers a model called "discrepant identity" where no uniformity of identity can be identified.[57] Instead, differences in degrees of compliance to Roman occupation can be identified through the material culture and religious practices. These scholars all focus on Romanization's problematic history that neglects agency first to the native population and second to the poor and less visible of society. Their concerns should not be taken lightly and indeed should shape any new conversations on the future of Romanization.

However, I believe that the term Romanization is not as antiquated as these scholars would suggest. Greg Woolf has revitalized the term simply by redefining it, noting

---

[54] Hingley 2008, 437.
[55] Chappell 2010, 89.
[56] Mattingly 2004, 9.
[57] Ibid., 9. He mentions on pages 10 and 11 a series of factors that could affect a person's social identity including: status, wealth, location, living under civil or martial law, being connected to the imperial government, employment, religion, origin, language or literacy, gender, and age.

that Romanization is still a "convenient shorthand" or "umbrella term" by which Roman/native interactions can be explored.[58] Rather than one culture subjugating another, Woolf argues that there is a social and cultural blending to create a new cultural system that is not purely native or Roman.[59] This simple distinction gives natives and the poor an agency in the process of cultural exchange that was denied to them within the traditional definition of Romanization and accounts for the bilateral acculturation that takes place between Rome and her provinces. I prefer to use the term Romanization for the same reasons Woolf does, namely that it is a convenient identifying term that, when defined correctly, can convey the complex process in a succinct manner. Further, I disagree that Romanization only allows archaeologists to see elites. Since elites are often the most visible archaeologically, this is a bias that all archaeologists face regardless of terminology.

Another approach to the issue of Romanization has been postulated by Jane Webster, who instead thinks that "Creolization" might be a better way to look at Roman/native relations in the provinces. She believes that the alternatives so far put forth in opposition to Romanization highlight the absence of Roman culture too much, and are just as polarizing as the traditional model of Romanization.[60] Webster believes that creolization, or blending two languages into a blended dialect, could be broadened to encompass the blending of two cultures such as Roman and native.[61] To me, Webster's model of Creolization addresses the same concerns as Woolf's model of Romanization, namely that both Romans and natives be given agency in the blending of cultures to form a new provincial culture that incorporates both Roman and native elements. Her model

---

[58] Woolf 1998, 7.
[59] Woolf 1997, 339.
[60] Webster 2001, 216.
[61] Ibid., 218.

renames this process, using a New World term to try to describe a process that began in the Old World. I see no reason to use a term meant to describe this New World blending of cultures when a simple redefinition of Romanization would suffice. In my interpretation, Romanization is the process by which Roman and native culture blend in order to create a wholly new provincial cultural identity.

Webster also notes that the blending of two cultures certainly leaves behind material evidence.[62] This evidence may be abundant in one place and non-existent in another. The archaeologist's job then is to identify this evidence, attempt to quantify it, and account for variables that might make it so abundant or non-existent. The main issue with such as study is that it can be troublingly subjective. How can one see Romanization in the archaeological record? Is some evidence more telling than other evidence? Does the archaeological evidence corroborate literary evidence? If not, are we missing something? What kind of variables might make seeing Romanization more challenging? Trying to quantify peoples' social and cultural identity will never be a hard science, but keeping these questions in mind during an exploration of evidence for Romanization will act as brakes on a car to restrict subjective opinion if there is no physical evidence.

Romanization can be identified in the archaeological record by the presence or absence of material culture that would indicate a blending of Roman and native culture. For example, perhaps there are copious clay figurines of a native goddess found in a Roman style temple. Maybe a temple in a province could have a traditionally native shape but be dedicated to a Roman god. Or individuals with non-Roman, native names could own a Roman villa, though we must be cautious assigning ethnicities to past people when we can't analyze their DNA. This then segues into the second issue, of assigning a merit

---

[62] Ibid.

system to the evidence. Not all evidence is created equally and sometimes only "bad" evidence can be recovered at a site, though these types of issues are eventualities on any archaeological excavation and must be born with patience.

Lastly, there is the obstacle in identifying why some areas reveal abundant evidence for Romanization and why others may not. The most obvious solution is that Romanization was a long-term process that happened differently and to different degrees throughout the Empire. Certain sites lack evidence of Romanization because the process failed to some degree there. The other solution is that the archaeologist could be missing evidence because of some outside force. This is clearly evident in the case of Dacia where excavators with political motives or needs throughout Romania's history have manipulated certain evidence to better suit political agendas, as evidenced by numerous Soviet era publications with clear nationalist or Marxist biases.[63]

Successful Romanization in Gaul

In Roman Gaul, Romanization was a long and arduous process which resulted in a successful bilateral acculturation, now referred to as Romano-Gallic culture. Romanization began during the conquest of Gallia Transalpina and was accelerated after Caesar conquered the rest of Gaul in the 50's BCE.[64] At this stage, it consisted mostly of Roman economic trade with the Gauls, since Roman objects were thought of us luxury goods only accessible to elites. There is a clear increase in the volume of trade during the end of the 2nd century BCE in southern Gaul. This economic relationship lent itself to Romanization after the full conquest of Gaul, since Gallic elites were increasingly interested in

---
[63] Otlean 2007, 5.
[64] King 1990, 43.

buying Roman goods. The Gallic *oppida*, or towns, were also run by a local government in a similar way to Roman towns, making the transition into Roman municipal governance easier.[65] The lack of large-scale resistance after the conquest, as evidenced in Britain, is owed to the nature of Rome's relationship with Gallic tribal elites. These warrior-elites had failed to defend Gaul from Roman invaders, and their positions in power were now precarious. They accepted Roman army appointments as officers of auxiliary units, meaning they were able to keep their status in this new society. Conversely, they were also Romanized into the rigid organization and bureaucracy of the Roman army. This in turn produced Gallic elites, removed from the conquest by only a generation, who were relatively loyal to Rome, integrated into Roman military and social life, and interested in buying Roman goods.[66]

Five Roman military colonies were created in southern Gaul before large-scale Roman monuments began to be erected after 30 BCE.[67] These settlements were located 115 km from each other, meaning most of the southern Gallic population was within one of these Roman spheres of influence.[68] By the reign of Augustus, southern Gaul had already been Romanized to a degree, making the integration of northern Gaul possible. The effects of Romanization are seen in the archaeological record at both Arausio (now modern Orange) and Lugdunum (now modern Lyon). Arausio, first colonized by legionary veterans around 35 BCE and called Julia Firma Secundanorum, was reestablished in the Flavian period as Flavia Tricastinorum.[69] Renaming the colony after the local Gallic

---

[65] Ibid., 65.
[66] Ibid.
[67] Narbo Martius Decumanorum at Narbonne, Arelate Sextanorum at Arles, Baeterrae Septimanorum at Beziers, Arausio Secundanorum at Orange, and Forum Julii Octavanorum at Frejus are the five colonies.
[68] Ebel 1988, 577.
[69] Dilke 1971, 159. The original sources for the Orange cadasters are Piganiol 1962 and Salviat 1977.

tribe, the Tricastini, was a sign that the tribe had received land distribution in the colony. This is seen in the Arausio *cadastre*, a stone map which represents the land surveyed at Arausio for tax exaction purposes.[70] The allocation of land specifically for the Gallic tribe shows both that the Gauls are now being further incorporated into city life and that they are still separate enough from the Roman population that they must be given separate land allotments. From the Roman perspective, renaming the colony was a meant to invite the Gauls into the city's life in order to tax them for land revenues. Thus, while the Gauls may have felt more included in Roman city life, the reason for their inclusion was purely economic.

In terms of material culture, Lugdunum provides clear evidence of the new Romano-Gallic culture emerging in the province. Lugdunum, created as a civilian settlement in 43 BCE and eventually became the procurator of Gallia Lugdunensis and Aquitania, the imperial mint for Gaul, and the altar of Rome and Augustus. Lugdunum became a hub of religious activity after the founding of cult worship of Rome and Augustus by Drusus on August 1, 12 CE.[71] A massive altar was built on the hill north of the Arar/Rhodanus river junction called the *Condate* in Celtic. The terrace was 150 feet long and the engineering and symbolism were Roman (winged Victories on columns and laurel wreaths on the altar), but it was placed in front of a sacred Gallic grove.[72] Another example of Celtic syncretism with Roman religious life is the Celtic temple plan constructed with Roman masonry techniques at La Tour de Vesone (Perigueux).[73] This temple retained the circular *cella* plan of earlier Celtic temples, but was most likely dedicated

---

[70] Ibid., 161.
[71] Drinkwater, 1983, 111-3.
[72] MacMullen 2000, 91.
[73] Drinkwater, 1983, 148.

to a Roman god. These examples of Roman and Gallic religion syncretizing highlight the increased Romanization of Gaul.

Gaul also highlights the spatial relationship between Roman cities and the effects of where Romanization on the provincial landscape. In Gaul, the Roman cities became flourishing centers of Roman and Gallic cultural exchange, with goods and ideas being traded. The cities of Gaul were where Romano-Gallic temples were first erected and where Gallic artistic styles melded with Roman construction techniques. In later centuries, Gaul is firmly Romanized, with Romano-Gallic culture evident even in smaller settlements such as at Ribemont-sur-Ancre, where a Romano-Celtic temple was the center of religious life for a town which began its life as an Iron Age Gallic settlement.[74] The archaeological record in Gaul indicates that Romanization was not only successful, but also that it stemmed first from Roman cities. However, this model for Romanization is not necessarily applicable to the province of Dacia.

Trajan's Dacian Campaigns

Dacia was already familiar with the Roman Empire when Trajan began to amass his legions for the first assault in 101 CE. The emperor Trajan (53-117 CE) was born Marcus Ulpius Traianus, the son of respectable Roman citizens living in the province of Hispania. He was adopted by his predecessor Nerva and became emperor upon Nerva's death in 98. Known as one of the Five Good Emperors, Trajan's is credited with extending the Roman Empire to its greatest size with his successive wars, while also increasing the prosperity and security of the Roman people. As outlined in Chapter 1, Decebalus had

---

[74] King 1990, 91.

been in negotiations with Domitian after the latter's Dacian War of 86-88 CE, which resulted in Domitian suing for peace with Decebalus and sending annual subsidies. According to Dio Cassius, Decebalus promptly used this money to fortify his territory against the Romans, perceiving that Roman pride would not allow his territory to remain independent.[75] Decebalus correctly assumed that Trajan saw Domitian's "defeat" as a disgrace and vowed to take the territory. Hanson and Hayes believe that Trajan's main motivator was border security on Rome's vulnerable Danubian front, where a growing Dacian presence under the singular rule of Decebalus was a real threat.[76] Whatever his reasons, Trajan is said to have marched 90,000 to 100,000 soldiers into Dacia in his two campaigns.[77]

The two successive campaigns into Dacia were short but brutal. Eutropius, who wrote the *Breviarium Historiae Romanae* in the 4th century CE, claimed that "Dacia enim diuturno bello Decibali viris fuerat exhausta" or "For Dacia had been exhausted of men during the long war with Decebalus".[78] Dan Rusco argued that the native Dacian elites were exterminated while the general population, though depleted, had not been wholly destroyed.[79] It is more likely that the elites, who would also have been the religious leaders and nobles found at Sarmizegetusa Regia, were killed off, while able-

---

[75] Dio Cassius, *Roman History*, 67.6.1.
[76] Ibid, pg 15. Scholars also mention the possibility that military glory or the mineral rich mountains of Dacia could also have been deciding factors for Trajan. E. Salmon (1936) disagrees that gold could have been a deciding factor in the 101-2 CE war, since Rome had long known of Dacia's mineral wealth and had not done much to exploit it before this time. He also asserts that gold in Dacia was not known to the Romans until they had already acquired the province. I think that there were many other factors (more immediate border control issues, lack of interest from different Emperors, lack of a sufficient legionary force) that prevented Rome from attempting to exploit Dacia's wealth before 101 and I assert that Dacia's wealth would have been one of several deciding factors in Trajan's decision to annex Dacia.
[77] Cupcea and Marcu 2006, 190. This included: "6 legions, 30 Praetorian cohorts, 14 alae, 34 cohortes, plus some expeditionary military corps from the Orient..." and "26 auxiliaries units were dislocated from Moesia Superior, 10 from Moesia Inferior, 6 from Pannonia, 3 units of Syria and another three from other provinces". Dio Cassius (*Roman History*, 67.7.2) puts the number closer to 100,000-150,000 men with 10-11 legions for the First War and 12 for the Second War.
[78] Eutropius, 8.6.2.
[79] Rusco 2004, 82.

bodied Dacian men were conscripted into the Roman army and Dacian women and children were taken as slaves. This scenario matches other evidence of how Rome dealt with conquered provinces and also neatly explains Trajan's claims of "extermination".

Another visual form of evidence for the Dacian Wars is Trajan's column. The monument's location was in the heart of Trajan's Forum in Rome, a gargantuan addition to the tradition of Imperial fora north of the Roman Forum. This splendid forum dwarfed the other Imperial fora, but was in clear communication with them aesthetically. Trajan's Forum connected on the west side to Augustus' Forum, following the lines of Caesar's forum to the south. Trajan's architect, Apollodorus of Damascus, blended the Greek agora, the Hellenistic sanctuary, and the traditional Roman forum to create this unique and imposing space.[80] The forum was entered through a tripartite monumental gateway, passing into a large courtyard surrounded by colonnades. On the far side of this courtyard was the Basilica Ulpia, an administrative buildings dedicated to law courts and commerce. It was the largest basilica in Rome, measuring 117 by 55 meters. From the basilica, a courtyard housed the Greek and Latin libraries, the temple to the deified Trajan (dedicated by Hadrian after his death), and the column. The column had a travertine foundation which supported the pedestal which was set marble facing. The monument was made up of 29 blocks of Luna marble, 8 for the plinth and pedestal and 19 for the column drums (Figure 8). On all four sides of the pedestal were friezes of amassed Dacian weapons to symbolize their subjugation (Figure 9).[81]

The column itself was, if unfurled, 200 meters in length, with the figures almost certainly brightly painted. It would have been crowned with a colossus of Trajan, but

---

[80] Packer 1997, 259-260.
[81] Ibid., 115.

since 1588 has been crowned by St. Peter. James Packer suggests that the scenes depicted on the column mirror Trajan's own literary account of the Dacian campaigns, now lost, which would have been housed in the adjacent libraries of Greek and Latin within the Forum of Trajan.[82] Of the 155 scenes depicted, Trajan features in 60 of them, with only 18 scenes dedicated to battles, and the rest showing the day-to-day mechanics of a military campaign.[83] As a life-long soldier, perhaps it is not a surprise that Trajan chose to depict the great power, determination, and diligence of the Roman army on his Dacian monument.

Fillipo Coarelli's volume on the column of Trajan provides several insights into these depictions. The narrative begins at the bottom of the column with preparations being made for the first campaign in 101 CE. Forts with provisions are amassed on the Roman side of the Danube before the river is crossed by a pontoon bridge. Fortifications are constructed, sacrifices are made, and Trajan himself addresses his army before they march deeper into Dacian territory. After several battles where the Dacians are routed and their towns destroyed, the column shows Decebalus suing for peace, an action which brings a close to the first Dacian War (Figure 10). Dio Cassius writes that,

> "ἐπεὶ δὲ ὁ Δεκέβαλος πολλὰ παρὰ τὰς συνθήκαςἀπηγγέλλετο α ὐτῷ ποιῶν, καὶ ὅπλα τεκατεσκευάζετο, καὶ τοὺς αὐτομολοῦντας ἐδέχετο, τάτε ἐρύματα ἐπεσκεύαζε, παρά τε τοὺς ἀστυγείτονας ἐπρεσβεύετο, καὶ τοῖς τἀναντία οἱ φρονήσασι πρότερον ἐλυμαίνετο..."[84]

---

[82] Ibid., 119.
[83] Ibid.
[84] Dio Cassius, Roman History, 68.10.3.

"After that Decebalus was reported to him(Trajan) to be going against the treaty in many things, for he was amassing arms, accepting deserters, readying defenses, sending ambassadors to his neighbors and maltreating those who had previously been against him..."

Thus the second campaign into Dacia was undertaken. This time, Trajan's masterful architect Apollodorus of Damascus engineered a bridge which Dio Cassius also describes and which the column faithfully represents (Figure 11). Dio Cassius says,

"Τραϊανὸς δὲ γέφυραν λιθίνην ἐπὶ τοῦ Ἴστρου κατεσκευάσατο, π ερὶ ἧς οὐκ ἔχω πῶς ἂν ἀξίως αὐτὸν θαυμάσω: ἔστι μὲν γὰρ καὶ τ ἄλλα αὐτοῦ ἔργα διαπρεπέστατα, τοῦτο δὲ καὶ ὑπὲρ ἐκεῖνα. ὡςγ ὰρ κρηπῖδές εἰσι λίθου τετραπέδου εἴκοσι, τὸ μὲν ὕψος πεντήκον τα καὶ ἑκατὸν ποδῶν πλὴν τῶν θεμελίων, τὸ δὲ πλάτος ἑξήκοντα : καὶ αὗται ἑβδομήκοντα καὶ ἑκατὸν ἀπ᾽ ἀλλήλων πόδας ἀπέχου σαι ἁψῖσι συνῳκοδόμηνται."[85]

"Trajan built a bridge of stone across the Ister (Danube), for which I do not hold in any way worthy enough praise. For distinguished are his other works, but this goes beyond them. For the pilings are twenty squares of stone one hundred and fifty feet in height above the foundation and sixty feet in width. And these, keeping one hundred and seventy feet from each other, are connected by arches."

This bridge seems to mark Trajan's intentions to annex the province rather than leave it in the hands of the client-king Decebalus. It is conjectured to have been built near the Iron Gates of Transylvania, a narrow gorge known for its strategic location in entering Dacia from the south over the Danube.[86] Further military preparations and battles take place, but in the panels that represent the Second Dacian War there is a distinct shift in the imagery. The Roman army climbs steadily upwards, conquering Dacian strongholds as they pursue the fleeing Dacians. The Dacians also move upwards, retreating in droves and

---

[85] Dio Cassius, *Roman History*, 68.13.1-2.
[86] Fodorean 2013, 19.

burning their forts behind them to leave nothing for their conquerors. Based on the column scenes alone, one could speculate that the razing of Sarmizegetusa Regia could have been performed by Decebalus' own troops rather than the Romans, though this cannot be corroborated. In any case, the final panels, though badly damaged, show Dacian refugees fleeing the Roman invaders with their families and livestock.

City Planning in 106 CE

The Second Dacian War from 105-6 CE led to the suicide of Decebalus, the razing of Sarmizegetusa Regia, and the subjugation of much of Decebalus' old territory. Trajan lost no time creating a Roman landscape in Dacia, including extending the road system he had begun before the Dacian Wars further into the province, stationing his legions at strategic positions, and establishing the first (and only) *colonia deducta* in Dacia, *Colonia Ulpia Traiana Augusta Dacica Sarmizegetusa*. He chose a "green-field" site, meaning no earlier native settlement had stood on the site. The chosen spot seems to have been strategic in several ways. First, it is halfway between the two main legionary forces in the province, stationed at Apulum and Berzobis. It was along two major commercial routes through Dacia, making it an economic as well as militarily advantageous site.[87] Furthermore, as Paul Zanker has explained, the city can be a symbolic representation of what (some) inhabitants wish it to portray, or "the notion of how a Roman imagined the idea city (or certain elements of this ideal city) ought to look".[88] For Trajan and the new colonial elites, naming the city after the old Dacian capital may have been an attempt at be-

---

[87] Cupcea and Marcu 2011, 252.
[88] Zanker 2000, 26.

ginning the process of Romanization, since the continued use of a native city name implies that Dacian culture might be welcome at this site.

The commercial and military position of the colony was carefully planned to exploit its position close to the main military garrisons and upon established trade routes. The new province was garrisoned by several legions, most notably the IIII Flavia at Berzobis and the XIII Gemina at Apulum.[89] Alan Diaconescu believes that legion IIII Flavia was used to build the new *colonia deducta* sometime between 106 and 110 since tiles with their stamp have been found at the earliest levels of construction.[90] Diaconescu vehemently opposes the proposal that the *colonia* was originally a legionary fort, suggesting instead that the timber foundations may have been part of earlier constructions such as a Roman marching camp burned in a 105 Dacian ambush and then parts of the "timber colony" erected on the site that preceded the colony's stone foundations of 109-110.[91]

There are several theories about the rationale behind Roman urban planning in the provinces and the high number of soldiers stationed in Dacia immediately following the conquest and an explanation for the impressively rapid Roman development in the new province.[92] A common theme in discussions of Roman urbanization is the use of the Roman *castrum* design as part of the overall city plan. Two theories emerged concerning the legionaries and the city plan at Sarmizegetusa. Either the city had begun as an actual Roman *castrum* and became part of the city center as the city grew in size; or the architectural plan of a *castrum* was simply adopted when erecting the new city center, most likely

---

[89] Cupcea 2013, 344. Cupcea mention that legion IIII Flavia may have been stationed at the site of Sarmizegetusa before being moved to its permanent residence at Berzobis, but recent excavations by Diaconescu have proven that the site did not hold a permanent legionary force before the creation of the city. Diaconescu 2004, 103.
[90] Diaconescu 2004, 89.
[91] Ibid., 103.
[92] Hayes and Hanson 2004, 15.

37

because the Romans planning the city were legionaries of the Roman army and most familiar with military architectural plans.[93] Several post-World War II scholars such as Dorin Alicu, Sorin Cocis, Constantin Ilies, and Alina Soroceanu suggested that there had been a legionary fort built on the site based on the style of the walled enclosure that made up the city center, which Diaconescu successfully challenged. While he has given substantial evidence that Sarmizegetusa was not built upon a legionary fort, Diaconescu notes that military style planning was obviously implemented when the site was first founded because the builders were familiar with and often specialists in military architecture.[94]

It has also been noted that the *forum* at Sarmizegetusa mirrors other examples in the provinces.[95] *Fora* of this type were found at Burnum in Dalmatia and Lopodunum in Germania, and they shared the same dimensions as Sarmizegetusa (Figure 12).[96] This suggests a shared model, which Diaconescu argues is used in both civilian and military contexts as it represented a wider "Hellenistic" architectural norm from the 2nd century BCE.[97] The *municipium* at Burnum was also founded under Trajan and its main entrance of the *forum* at Burnum and Sarmizegetusa both measure 5.60 meters across, the secondary entrances measure 3.55 meters across, and the width of the nave is 17.85 meters across at both.[98] The shared architectural plan for creating a *forum* is another piece of evidence that the builders of Sarmizegetusa were from the ranks of the Roman military,

---

[93] Zanker 1998, 27.
[94] Diaconescu 2004, 103.
[95] Zanker 1998, 94.
[96] Diaconescu 2004, 94.
[97] Ibid.
[98] Ibid.

strengthening the argument that the first settlers of the colony were probably veterans of the Dacian Wars, though other settlers would come later from other parts of the Empire.

This shared plan highlights Dacia's position in Trajan's grander architectural scheme. Trajan not only extended the borders of the Roman Empire, but he made sure that everyone knew about his exploits by carving them in stone. Once the riches of conquered territories were accessible to him, Trajan embarked on a remarkable building program at home and abroad. In Rome, Trajan built his mammoth forum which dwarfed Caesar's and Augustus' nearby fora. The forum housed his column, a temple, libraries, and a grand equestrian statue of himself. The forum abutted the markets, a three-story shopping mall which doubled as a retaining wall for the earth that had been cut away from the Esquiline hill to make room for his massive forum. His great baths, which replaced portions of Nero's Domus Aurea on the Esquiline Hill, were also done on a grand scale which emphasized the great wealth acquired from the Dacian Wars and also Trajan's propagandistic campaign to beautify Rome.

His building program extended to the provinces as well, as evidenced by the speed with which his new *colonia deducta* in Dacia was monumentalized. For example, the defensive walls of the colony were quickly built of grey-greenish sandstone from the nearby quarry at Pesteana.[99] Along with standardized building plans, Trajan extended his reach into his new province with an impressive road construction program which Florin Fodorean suspects followed several pre-Roman trade routes through the province.[100] That Sarmizegetusa is equidistant between the two legionary camps of the province is seen as

---

[99] Diaconescu 2004, 91.
[100] Fodorean 2013, 15.

evidence of Trajan's early mapping of the province and accurate understanding of the existing road system.[101]

All of Trajan's building projects after the Dacian Wars indicate his intent to include Dacia as the newest province of his Empire. The province was rich in gold, minerals, stone, and agricultural land. Here was the sort of prize Trajan would have hoped for. It made him personally wealthy while also adding to the economic strength of the Empire. It offered new land for retiring army veterans and most of all it created an added buffer against the wild barbarians of the northern Danubian region. In Rome's eyes Dacia must have looked like any other conquered province -- one ready to be Romanized. The remainder of this study will look to evaluate the extent to which they succeeded.

Chapter 3: A Roman City in Dacia

<u>City Engineering</u>

Roman colonization under the Empire took on different features from the Republican method of colonization, mainly because Roman rule was more fully established un-

---

[101] Ibid., 17.

der the Empire and the settlers of these colonies were mostly ex-soldiers in the Roman army. In the Republic, *coloniae Latinae* (colonies of non-citizens) and *coloniae civium Romanorum* (colonies of citizens) were established in different locations. *Coloniae Latinae* were established farther from Rome and were often larger, offering more land to settlers but less protection from the Roman state against invasions, their size being meant to protect them. *Coloniae civium Romanorum* were established near Rome to keep legal citizens close enough to participate in the legal proceedings that were their right.[102]

During the Empire, this was no longer necessary, since most colonies began as *militares* (military camps) or as *municipii* (native towns incorporated into Roman rule that were allowed to keep their former governing apparatus in place).[103] The colonists of these settlements were discharged legionaries who were provided with land upon their retirement as a sort of pension from the Roman state, which also doubled as a way to integrate career soldiers back into civilian life. As ex-legionaries, these men were more easily able to defend themselves against hostile forces, and with the added support of permanent legionary camps in a province, these colonies thrived. The colony established at Sarmizegetusa was a veteran *militares* colony, which fits into the overall picture of Trajan's Dacian conquest. Trajan and his veterans would have seen the establishment of this type of colony as standard Roman practice, since the land allotments handed out would have been used as veteran's pensions. To the Romans, the main purpose of the establishment of this colony was a means of exploiting more land and resources for the benefit of the Empire, rather than as a means of civilizing their defeated barbarian foes.

---

[102] Salmon 1970, 16.
[103] Ibid., 145.

By the Empire, Romans had a universal system in place for the creation of new colonies, both military and civilian in origin. First, *agrimensores* or land surveyors were sent out to get an understanding of the topography and choose the site for the new colony.[104] Literary records show that Romans had very little knowledge of the topography, climate, or geography of Dacia before Trajan's conquest.[105] Julius Caesar's *De Bello Gallico* was one of the first texts to describe the peoples that made up the tribes north of the Danube, and he mentions that the land beyond the Dacian homeland was uncharted territory.[106] As discussed in the previous chapter, the *agrimensores* chose a site for Sarmizegetusa that had no previous Dacian settlement, and was along established trade routes. Any knowledge of Dacian topography would have been gleaned during the Dacian Wars by the military surveyors. Though it is not known when the military encampments of Apulum and Berzobis were established, the placement of Sarmizegetusa directly between the two is doubtlessly intentional, suggesting an early date for these camps. G. Cupcea and F. Marcu have done a topographic survey of Sarmizegetusa and its environs which have shown that the specific location may also have been chosen partially for its hygienic value, since rain water would drain down the slope of the hill of the city.[107] Since the colony was originally meant as a veteran colony, the *agrimensores* would have measured out land allotments for each colonist, a process called *centuriation*, evidence for which can be seen from air photographs today (Figure 13).[108] These units

---

[104] Ibid., 20.
[105] Herodotus, *The Histories*, 5.10.1. Herodotus is dubious that bees could live north of the Danube because he is positive it is too cold for bees or humans to live there.
[106] Fodorean 2013, 9.
[107] Cupcea, G., F. Marcu 2011, 546.
[108] Ibid., 547.

were all equally measured plots of land meant to be a pension for military retirees around the main settlement of the city.

The urban plan of the city is the best evidence to prove a *limitatio* for Sarmizegetusa. The distance between *cardo maximus* and *decumanus maximus* from the perceived *locus gromae* (in the middle of the *forum*) were measured. The length between the cardines was 35.50 meters or 1 *actus*. The distance between the *decumanus maximus* and the only other *decumanus* identifiable was 71 meters or 2 *actus*.[109] This 2 x 1 *actus* unit proves that Sarmizegetusa was built on a specific grid system. Further evidence of this is that the later Severan plan, which added two extra *insulae* blocks to the west, seems to also follow these measurements. Outside of the city, the orientation of the land allotments is west of north and can be seen to the north, east, and south of the city.[110] Modern roads helpfully often follow the directions of the ancient Roman roads and these roads are 120 *pedes* (Roman feet) or multiples of an *actus*.[111] From the 3rd century a 20 x 20 actus land division system can be seen through orthophotos, or photographs that can be used as maps because they have a uniform-scale and georectified (Figure 14). From the city center, an area of 6 x 11 km has been observed that follows a full Roman *cadastre* system rather than just a *limitatio*. This is seen both through the orthophoto maps and the modern roads, which are all equal distances either as an *actus* or multiples of an *actus* to each other.[112] The second land division orientation seen on the orthophoto maps to the east may be evidence that not all of the area around Sarmizegetusa was centuriated at the

---

[109] Ibid., 551.
[110] Ibid., 552.
[111] Ibid.
[112] Ibid., 553.

same time. The full extent of the *limitatio* is still unknown at Sarmizegetusa, though the orthophoto maps indicate that there were two separate *extra-murus* orientations.

The *centuriation* of the city was closely tied to the extensive road-building project, which would have been happening simultaneously. The road system was ongoing during both Dacian campaigns and as the army pushed further into Dacian territory, they left impressive imperial roads behind them.[113] Both the roads and the *centuriation* of settlements would have been undertaken by the same army who had invaded the province and were highly trained in the construction of bridges, roads, and buildings. Their expertise in construction continued to be helpful once they retired from the army, since they would need these skills to build their new homesteads and the city. The city layout was not left up to chance either, since a uniform *castrum* style layout for new cities had been adopted even during Augustan expansion. The *castrum* design was therefore able to account for all the major architectural components that were considered necessary for a Roman city, the most important of which was the *forum*.

The *forum* was the civic center of the city, displaying virgin site origins, meaning the site was free from any prior use by Dacians.[114] Diaconescu constructs a compelling argument for the evolution of the urban center's *forum*. The public buildings of the first Trajanic *forum* on the site were made of wood, measured 46.30 x 42.00 meters, and were probably erected around the colony's founding in 106 to 108 AD. Through Diaconescu's excavations, he determined that the timber structures found under the later Trajanic *forum* were civilian in nature rather than of any military affiliation.[115] He draws this conclusion from excavations undertaken from 1989 to 1994 in the area of the *forum*. Beneath the

---

[113] Fodorean 2013, 15.
[114] Haynes and Hanson, 2004, 18.
[115] Diaconescu 2004, 97-9.

stone *forum*, excavators discovered remains of a smaller wooden *forum*. This *forum* was destroyed and a larger stone *forum* was built over it. However, a layer of military paraphernalia was discovered as well, prompting speculation that this was the site of the military camp. However, burnt wood, tent-nails, 98 Trajanic coins, pierced plates of armor, and shot arrowheads were found, but no earthen walls or tiles with military stamps which would be indicative of a permanent military installation.[116]

Diaconescu thus believes that while the remains of a small auxiliary force stationed at the site in 105 CE may have been uncovered, there is no evidence that a legionary camp ever existed at Sarmizegetusa. Still, there is evidence that there could have been a gap of 1 to 2 years between the end of the Second Dacian War and the establishment of Sarmizegetusa as a colony. Iulius Sabinus may have been governor of Dacia before Terentius Scaurianus, who was the founder of Sarmizegetusa and generally believed to be the first governor of Dacia starting in 109.[117] It is unlikely that during this time Sarmizegetusa was left unoccupied due to its general strategic importance midway between the legionary camps of Apulum and Berzobis. This again left doubt in excavators' minds that a military camp could have been set up before the city was laid out.

However, Diaconescu was able to prove that the *insulae* south of the forum excavated from 1995 to 1999 were civilian in nature and lacked any military affiliations. The civilian nature of the *insulae* is discussed in greater length below. Since their constructions phases mirrored those of the *forum*, it was clear that the colonists were not repurposing previous military buildings as houses, proving that Sarmizegetusa was civilian in nature from its inception. Under Trajan, the buildings of the *forum* were expanded and

---

[116] Ibid., 96.
[117] Ibid., 97.

refinished in stone, and the dimensions of this forum match other *fora* built under Trajan and Hadrian in frontier zones, suggesting a set building formula.[118] This model of upgrading the existing timber public buildings into stone is a Trajanic addition that indicates the position of Sarmizegetusa as a provincial capital.

The *insulae* that have been excavated show that the transition from a wood to stone *forum* forced some of the original *insulae* to be torn down to accommodate the larger stone structure.[119] Some of the excavations of these *insulae* have revealed Mediterranean atrium-style houses with a central court surrounded by a peristyle (Figure 15). Peristyle homes had numerous rooms surrounding a courtyard which was ringed by a peristyle, or walkway. This style of house had become the norm in Roman towns since it fit well into the orthogonal city plan. However, other homes called corridor houses were also excavated. Corridor houses are generally long, rectangular structures with one long corridor through which the rooms on either side can be entered. Diaconescu claims that these are typical of native dwellings and are popular in the Rhineland and the upper Danube provinces.[120] In any case, the *insulae* contained several different structures per block, with a corridor house and two atrium style houses being positively identified in one block.[121] The findings of these excavations have further supported Diaconescu's claim that the site of Sarmizegetusa was not originally a military fort and therefore was always planned to be a colony.

---

[118] Ibid., 94.
[119] Ibid., 98.
[120] Ibid., 98-9. Otlean notes that many Dacian houses were circular or rectangular with very few rooms. In Figure 16, one house that has multiple rooms with doorways in a straight line down the middle can be seen, but I would hesitate to label this a corridor house.
[121] Ibid., 98.

As mentioned in chapter one, the temples at Sarmizegetusa are all housed in the *area sacra* at the northern end of the city.[122] This area yields no remnants of old Dacian religious beliefs, as noted by Rusco, which again emphasizes the lack of any religious blending between the colonists and local Dacians.[123] Mihailescu-Birliba indicates that several foreign deities from all over the Empire were introduced to Dacia through the Roman colonists at Sarmizegetusa. For example, Aur. Laecanius Paulinus, a Decurion of Sarmizegetusa, built an altar for Deus Sol Ierhabol, a Palmyrean deity.[124] These sorts of funerary monuments were found throughout the city and were dedicated to numerous gods from all over the Empire, highlighting both the multi-nationality of the gods the colonists worshipped both within and outside the Roman pantheon, and the distinct lack of any native Dacian gods in the epigraphic evidence. Being a veteran military colony, Mithras was an important deity, along with Nemesis, Silvanus, and Serapis.[125] Having the temple precinct outside of the main enclosure of the city allowed the orthogonal plan to lie undisturbed by awkward temple orientations, such as the Aesculapius and Hygeia precinct.

The amphitheatre at Sarmizegetusa was also originally made of timber, dated by numismatic evidence between the years of 109 and 112 and 119 and 121 CE (Figure 17).[126] This was a transitional period between Trajan and Hadrian and was an early example of Roman affluence in the city, as an amphitheatre denotes the adoption of Roman culture through the architectural design, the activities that took place there, and the peo-

---

[122] Otlean, 2007, 165.
[123] Dan Rusco, 2004, 81.
[124] Mihailescu-Birliba, 8.
[125] Otlean 2007, 187.
[126] Diaconescu 2004, 99-100.

ple it attracted.[127] The first amphitheatre was mostly made of wood with stone used to construct the stone wall for the arena and two *tribunalia*, or reserved seating areas. Ioan Piso estimates that the amphitheatre could hold around 5,000 spectators at a time.[128] Diaconescu insists that there is military influence evident in building techniques in both the forum and the amphitheatre, which suggests a Roman reliance on military engineers for most building projects, rather than the military use of the structures in question.[129] The necessity of an amphitheater is not immediately understood, since a grand entertainment structure would seem to be superfluous and excessive for such a new colony. However, recalling the Trajanic and Hadrianic coins found in conjunction with the wooden phase of the amphitheatre, its early construction date shows that this building was important for Roman-style entertainment that was necessary for establishing Roman cultural identity in their new landscape.

The Roman governmental buildings at Sarmizegetusa for the financial procurator and the governor were some of the first excavated and were found in the northeast region of the main enclosure. As the *colonia deducta*, Sarmizegetusa was the center of the political and financial offices of the province. The most powerful man in the province, the provincial governor, would have resided here at least under Trajan and continued to be the seat of the financial procurator of the province (Figure 18).[130] These offices were essential to the running not only of the city but the overall province, making Sarmizegetusa a nucleus of wealthy inhabitants. The public sectors of the city would have been teeming

---

[127] Ibid., 100.
[128] Piso 2006, 444.
[129] Ibid., 103.
[130] Otlean 2007, 165. Excavations at Apulum have identified the governor's palace near to the *municipium*. In the later years of the province, Apulum seems to have eclipsed Sarmizegetusa in importance both administratively and economically, as evidenced by Hadrian's reorganization of the provinces.

with lawyers, land surveyors, tax collectors, and other important officers, ensuring that the province continued to operate properly.

The main components of a Roman city are all found here at Sarmizegetusa. A forum for conducting business, governmental buildings for the governor and other top officials, an amphitheatre for entertainment, temples for the gods, and *insulae* for the colonists. If the name of the city was omitted, it is easy to see that this could be any Roman city throughout the Empire, lacking any markers that this specific city was found in Dacia. Thus this city can be said to be a properly Romanized city, since its inhabitants were not from Rome themselves but took on Roman cultural identities that marked their spatial habitat. A lack of local architectural influences, however, does not mean that Dacian culture was not present in the urban center. An analysis of material culture must be conducted to establish cultural identity at the site.

A Local Production Center

Regardless of whether the abundant resources of Dacia were factors in Trajan's decision to campaign there, these resources were quickly exploited especially at Sarmizegetusa (Figure 19). Trajan wasted no time in mining gold and iron from the Apuseni Mountains, as well as surface extraction centers such as Hunedoara, Teliucu Inferior, Ruda, Ghelar, Alun, and Almasu Mic.[131] Recent rescue excavations, aerial photography, and land survey have revealed several of these Roman production sites.[132] These vast quantities of metals were used to pay for the expensive wars and to finance Trajan's building projects both in Rome and abroad in his newly won province. The marble used

---

[131] Ibid., 181.
[132] Ibid.

to quickly transform Sarmizegetusa from a city of wood to one of stone was quarried only 11 km from the city at Bucova near the Iron Gates and the marble quarried at Bucova traveled as far as Apulum.[133] Limestone at Sarmizegetusa was from the Iordachel valley to the west of the city and a sandstone quarry nearby can be hypothesized since it was used extensively in Trajanic buildings.[134] While the mining of gold and iron was extensive through much of Dacia, it is curious that some areas known previously by native Dacians as profitable were no longer exploited and seem abandoned during Roman occupation, such as the iron reserves in the Orastie Mountains near the old Dacian capital of Sarmizegetusa Regia.[135] The Romans seem to have favored the lowlands in Dacia throughout their occupation, and their unfavorable feelings towards the area surrounding Sarmizegetusa Regia (which the Romans razed to the ground in 106) may explain the shift away from mining and quarrying industries in the area. More likely, however, is that mines and quarries located closer to Sarmizegetusa were simply more convenient.

The buildings of the city vary in construction material and style. The main *forum* walls were made up of mostly limestone or sandstone blocks in *opus quadratum*, and were mostly used as a decorative and monumentalizing element while also bearing heavy weight.[136] Most buildings in Sarmizegetusa and in Roman Dacia are built using *opus incertum*, where irregular shaped stones are inserted into a core of *opus caementicium*, a mixture of small stones and lime. This technique was used for many buildings because the materials used are readily available and cheap to transport.[137] In terms of stylistic dif-

---

[133] Ibid., 183.
[134] Ibid., 184.
[135] Ibid., 182. Sarmizegetusa is only 40 km from Sarmizegetusa Regia, so the mine would have been fairly accessible to the Romans.
[136] Alicu 1995, 27.
[137] Ibid., 29.

ferences, several different column bases, columns, and capitals were used. Tuscan and Ionic bases are attested, made of marble and limestone. A third style of base is attested which is found nowhere else in the world, consisting "of a square plinth supporting a cylindrical segment followed by a truncated cone out near the base".[138] The column drums themselves are not well preserved, with only 8 of 17 original drums intact now. None of these follow the Tuscan or Corinthian order proportions, indicating an emulation of classical models that the provincial artists were not fully able to adhere to.[139] Lastly, there is one example of a Greek Doric capital, whereas there are 20 examples of the Roman Doric style. Only one true Ionic capital has been found at Sarmizegetusa, with 26 examples of Corinthian capitals, most of which are associated with the temple of Liber Pater and the large unnamed temple. Two composite style capitals were also found; an amalgamation of Corinthian and Ionic style are Figure 20).[140]

It seems that Roman funerary stelae were locally manufactured from stone at Sarmizegetusa and burials, usually cremations, were located outside of the city along major roads.[141] A study of funerary stelae in Dacia, done by Luca Bianchi, states that the art of these funeral stelae for Roman colonists indicates the creation of these monuments began as soon as the city began to get access to the stone quarry at Bucova, 12 km west of Sarmizegetusa, around 108-9 CE.[142] The sculptural evidence at Sarmizegetusa has been compiled into a catalogue by Dorin Alicu, Constantin Pop, and Volker Wollman of 551 securely identified items and 108 which are now lost or unidentifiable. Several of these items undoubtedly came from the small sculptural workshop discovered within the enclo-

---

[138] Ibid., 35.
[139] Ibid.
[140] Ibid., 36.
[141] Otlean 2007, 190.
[142] Bianchi 1985, 171.

sure for the temples dedicated to Aesulapius and Hygeia. It consists of a stone platform 3 square meters and large quantities of marble chippings were found on and around the platform.[143] Its size and location suggest that it created ritual votives for worshipers of the gods. Though this particular workshop is small, quality and likeness of several stone monuments from Sarmizegetusa indicate that several workshops were found in the city, and there was likely a local school of sculpture.

Several different materials were used to create the monuments found at Sarmizegetusa. The authors of the catalogue used petrological and mineralogical analyses on 42 pieces.[144] The quarry at Bucova supplied the marble for the site, while grit-stones were used for a large number of works, such as funerary monuments, altars, and stelae.[145] Grit-stone deposits existed in almost every direction around Sarmizegetusa, making it easily accessible. Limestone was used for buildings as well as monuments, and limestones quarries are also located in several directions around the site, though they are farther than grit-stone quarries.[146] It is clear that the Romans exploited numerous natural stone deposits around the site for their buildings and monuments and imported marble, as the debris in the workshop shows, again indicating that there was a healthy population of workshops in the city.

As noted above, there was a workshop within the Aesculapius and Hygeia sanctuary, and 17 pieces depict either the god, the goddess, or both together. Numerous other gods from both the Greco-Roman and the Oriental or Egyptian pantheons are depicted, including Liber Pater, Minerva, Nemesis, Silvanus, Venus, Cybele, Mithras, Isis and Ser-

---

[143] Alicu et al. 1979, 3.
[144] Ibid., 5.
[145145] Ibid. Grit-stone consists of lime, clayey, ferrous, micaceous, and fossiliferous minerals. It is hard and relatively fracture resistant but easy to work, making it an economic alternative to marble.
[146] Ibid., 6.

apis. In terms of local Danubian deities, the cult of the Danubian riders is attested by several reliefs at Sarmizegetusa. This Danubian cult developed in Dacia and Moesia during the 2nd century CE.[147] Another local god Heros, the Thracian horseman, has 7 reliefs and some local variation in depicting the god Silvanus is noted.[148] Dacians did not generally depict their gods, which makes any identification of deities as local dubious. Therefore, while there is a notable provincial style being employed in Dacia, sculptural decoration doesn't seem to be excessively helpful in identifying a particularly Dacian presence at Sarmizegetusa rather than a general Danubian influence.

In terms of funerary stelae, a majority of the residents at Sarmizegetusa chose draped statues that were mass-produced from a city workshop and there is even a name associated with one of these statues, Claudius Saturnius (Figure 21).[149] Other funeral monuments were more elaborate, such as the mausoleum of the Aurelli family discovered by Constantine Daicoviciu in 1934, which was a Roman brick burial monument located 600 meters northeast of the main site (Figure 22). Within the mausoleum near the sarcophagus of a young girl, most likely the child of "Q. Aurelius Tertius" who owned the tomb, there were clay vessels, glass vessels, a bracelet, a coin dating to the reign of Antoninus Pius, and a rotten wooden box that contained rouge.[150] The finds themselves are significant because they are typically Roman grave goods and the coin confidently dates the monument to an early period in the life of the city, around 142 CE.

Local resources used in the production of Roman funerary monuments seems to have remained a constant throughout the city's history and is another example of the

---

[147] Ibid., 21.
[148] Silvanus had his own temple at Sarmizegetusa and seems quite popular, suggesting he may have been assimilated with a local god.
[149] Ibid., 4.
[150] Daicoviciu 1944, 44-5.

many uses of Dacian stone resources at Sarmizegetusa. These monuments included dedicatory inscriptions and sarcophagi. Since many of the inhabitants of Sarmizegetusa were originally from other provinces within the Roman Empire, their monuments blended traditional Roman religious and iconographic motifs with their own motifs.[151] A study done by Carmen Ciongradi notes that there are influences from both the East, mainly Palmyra by way of Aquileia and Intercisa, and the West, mainly from Northern Italy by way of Pannonia.[152] Ciongradi concludes that both influences are possible, but that the style chosen for a funerary monument depended on the status of the settlement, whether the person was civilian or military, the origins of the artisans who create the monument, and the taste of the particular customer.[153] The use of stone at Sarmizegetusa was extensive and it is assumed that the stone was carved on site after it journeyed from the quarry. Otlean has created two distribution maps that show the shift in industrial activity throughout Dacia from pre-Roman conquest to Roman activity (Figures 23 and 24). These maps demonstrate a shift in mining and quarrying from sites near native Dacian settlements to sites closer to Roman settlements after the invasion.

Accordingly, other production centers also cropped up quickly at Sarmizegetusa including pottery production centers as well as glass, bronze, and iron smelting workshops, which indicate that Sarmizegetusa was relatively self-sufficient in terms of manufacture.[154] The pottery at Sarmizegetusa suggests a local origin for clay acquisition, but the forms found in the city are distinctly Roman.[155] Alicu *et al.*'s catalogue contains 167 vessels, both fragmentary and whole with five examples of *terra sigillata*, some moulds,

---

[151] Ciongradi 2004, 169.
[152] Ibid.
[153] Ibid., 177.
[154] Otlean 2007, 182.
[155] Alicu 1994, 77.

spinning whorls, beads, and 6 *lararia* or portable ritual altars.[156] The criterion for the organization of the catalogue was based on the shape of the vessels and their functionality, and pottery was reportedly recovered from multiple contexts including the forum, tombs, *villae rusticae*, temples, and the amphitheatre. Several of the *terra sigillata* vessels were provenanced to specific workshops, including one bowl from a workshop in Lavoye, France and others were Arretine.[157] Both fine ware and cooking ware were identified in the catalogue, and the moulds in the collection provide evidence for mould-made pottery production at the site. The portable altars were hand-made, but the majority of the vessels in the catalogue would have been wheel-made. All of the items represented in the Alicu *et al.* catalogue are Roman in design, though the clay used to make the pottery would be local. The evidence, which includes imported Roman pottery, locally produced Roman pottery, and pottery kiln sites, seems to indicate that Roman colonists were producing local pottery at Sarmizegetusa. The absence of identified native pottery at Sarmizegetusa seems troubling, since it is found elsewhere at Roman sites throughout Dacia.

Other ceramic objects found in Roman archaeological contexts were stamped lamps. There have been over 71 lamps excavated with 14 initials or names stamped on them (Figure 25).[158] The stamps on the lamps and their material characteristics have separated them into four categories: productions of Italian or Greek workshops, imitations of Italian products and products of other provinces, imitations an original products manufactured in different cities of Dacia, and imitations and original products made in Sarmizegetusa.[159] The first type is distinguished by its fine fabric, its quality of temper

---

[156] Ibid., 125-139.
[157] Ibid., 139, Ciongradi 2004, 174.
[158] Alicu and Nemes 1977, 9.
[159] Ibid.

and firing, and its brick-red color with a red paste.[160] These date to the 2nd century CE, the time right after the creation of the city. Another category of lamps matched the mould sizes of moulds from Pannonia, a province of Rome which borders Dacia to the west, and they indicate active trade with Sarmizegetusa and Pannonia.[161] The last category of lamps, which are found in large quantities in similar archaeological contexts, must have been of local production, furthering the argument that Sarmizegetusa was relatively self-sufficient in terms of producing ceramics.[162] Lamps were discovered from several different archaeological contexts at Sarmizegetusa. Large quantities were found in the *area sacra*, suggesting that they were given as offerings to the gods or that there was a ceramic workshop near the cult area. Others were found in the *forum* and the *insulae* blocks. However, many more were found in uncertain contexts or are now housed in museums with incomplete catalogues of their artifacts, which makes provenancing these lamps impossible.

Mircea Negru, who has created a typology of native Dacian pottery, argues that the absence of native pottery in urban centers of Dacia like Sarmizegetusa was not an outright sign that no natives lived in the urban centers. Instead Negru argues that ceramic production levels at large urban centers before the conquest, such as at Sarmizegetusa Regia, were negligible as well, implying that pottery production wasn't a large part of urban life in Iron Age Dacia. Further complicating the issue is that several Roman forms such as hand-made bowls, plates, and lids were already used in Dacia prior to Roman occupation. The hand-made pottery in Dacia must then be carefully analyzed, since attributing a native or Roman origin to the pottery can be problematic. The overall life of a pot

---

[160] Ibid.
[161] Ibid., 11.
[162] Ibid.

must also be taken into account when discussing pottery. Pottery can be made by an individual with a certain social identity but then sold to someone with a different social identity. To see this identity exchange in the pottery is nearly impossible. The nature of identity and pottery has long been discussed as a fluid process that requires multiple levels of analysis to parse. Therefore, until positive evidence of native Dacian pottery is found at Sarmizegtusa, the pottery at Sarmizegetusa must be assumed to be produced by Roman colonists for consumption by Roman colonists, but possibilities of cross-cultural exchange, emulation, and assimilation of styles should not be overlooked.

Native pottery in Dacia has been attested since the first explorations of ancient sites were undertaken in the country. From the first excavations, it is clear that Roman and Dacian pottery were found at similar sites, often ones which were first occupied during the Roman period. Roman camps seem to have been places of greater exchange of ceramics, since Dacian pottery has been found at fourteen Roman camps and four civilian settlements of Roman camps.[163] This overlap between local and Roman pottery seems to indicate the sort of cultural blending that Romanization is supposed to produce and which was lacking at Sarmizegetusa.

Negru's typology combines functionality with the shape of the vessel, and he indicates that the vessels are either for food storage, table ware, illumination vessels, or kitchen vessels.[164] The typology consisted of 175 hand-made vessels and 21 wheel-made vessels. The paste usually contained sand and mica, sometimes with gravel or limestone, though the quality of paste differs from vessel to vessel.[165] The wheel-made vessels needed to be carefully analyzed, since it was possible that some of these vessels were actually

---

[163] Negru 2003, 71.
[164] Ibid., 10.
[165] Ibid., 29.

Roman provincial production rather than Dacian made. The distinction between provincial pottery and local was made by study of the paste composition and color.[166]

The typology is able to catalogue the vessels by manufacturing technique as well as body shape, allowing them to be studied not only for their intended purpose but also for the technology Dacian potters used as opposed to Roman potters. In general, Negru notes that native hand-made pottery is found most frequently in rural areas of the province such as settlements, cemeteries, and *villae rusticae* to the eastern side of the province. The east of the province is generally considered to be less populated, either because it really was or because ancient sources call it the *"terra deserta"* or "deserted land" which was used as a buffer zone against invading tribes.[167] It seems that in less urban areas of Dacia, local pottery traditions were continued into the Roman occupation and even after, with Dacian pottery being identified in contexts from the Iron Age to after the Romans abandon the province in 275 CE. This sort of continuity suggests that native Dacians continued to produce pottery using local technology and styles in rural areas despite the introduction of Roman pottery to the market.

Metal production at Sarmizegetusa has also been identified. In terms of iron artifacts, goldsmith, blacksmith, carpenters, and agricultural tools have been excavated throughout the site and numerous building materials such as nails, closing mechanisms for doors, and links have been found.[168] Other metal objects recovered include spoons, hooks, knives, candlesticks, slate-pencils (writing implements), harness paraphernalia, wagon objects, and weapons including swords, spearheads, and arrowheads.[169] Bronze

---

[166] Ibid., 23.
[167] Ellis 1998, 225.
[168] Alicu et al. 1994, 11-20.
[169] Ibid., 26-36.

artifacts included broaches, military equipment, harness equipment, ornaments and jewelry, medical instruments, toilet and cosmetic instruments, and furniture accessories.[170] These accoutrements are indicative of metalworking workshops and excavations have found evidence of smelting furnaces within the city.[171] Not all of these items would have been produced at Sarmizegetusa. For instance, most of the military finds would have come with the legionaries from various provenances. However, the wealth of artifacts along with the archaeological evidence for metalworking points to Sarmizegetusa as home to a thriving community of artisans.

A final example of production at Sarmizegetusa is glass manufacturing. So far this craft, along with iron metallurgy, seem to have been performed outside the main enclosure at the site, though Otlean points out that very few *insulae* inside the enclosure have been excavated, so this trend may be due to lack of evidence. Several glass vessels were found in the Mausoleum of the Aurelii and all seem to be made locally; their quality doesn't indicate any importation from a well-known Western workshop and suggests the presence of a local glass workshop at Sarmizegetusa.[172] This has led Alicu *et al.* to believe that there were specialty workshops in the city for this kind of craftsmanship. Alicu *et al.* has 34 entries in his catalogue of glass finds at Sarmizegetusa, most of which are *unguentaria*, which are small glass bottles most often used for storing liquids or powders.[173] The six vessels found in the Mausoleum of the Aurelii are dated to around 142 CE, the date of the inscription for Q. Aurelius Tertius. The glass beads in the catalogue may have come from a specialized workshop at Tibiscum, a town not far from

---

[170] Ibid., 47-56.
[171] Otlean 2007, 165.
[172] Ibid., 71-2.
[173] Ibid. Some other objects include jugs, cups, plates, bowls, beads, and a fragment of a *guttus* or baby feeding bottle.

Sarmizegetusa.[174] Alicu mentions that a neutron activation analysis would be forthcoming, but no such publication has appeared. All of these types of production, from stone carving to iron working to glass blowing, show that Sarmizegetusa was a vital center of Romanized production in the new province. All of these types of production begin early in the city's history and provide a key link to Roman culture elsewhere in the Empire for these newly arrived colonists. Sarmizegetusa, through the evidence of metal and pottery imports, seems to have been well-linked to the rest of the Empire's economic apparatus by the extensive road system built by Trajan, which allowed it to function as any other cosmopolitan city of the time.

Roman Depictions of Dacians

In correlation with the archaeological remains, which show a distinctly Roman cultural expression at Sarmizegetusa, it is also important to examine the way Romans saw the native Dacians with whom they were possibly sharing land now. There is an abundance of Roman artistic representations of Dacians under Trajan thanks to his impressive building program in Rome, which included his forum, markets, baths, and of course his column depicting his Dacian campaigns. The column erected in the center of his forum is the most noteworthy in its abundance of representations of Dacians (Figure 26). Dacians are shown as a distinct ethnic group, according to I. M. Ferris, though their armor and weapons are not distinctly different.[175] They wear pants and caps and carry oval shields. Ferris notes that the overall tone of the frieze on the column is a contrast between the civility and order of the advancing Roman units, who build bridges and roads as they

---
[174] Ibid.
[175] Ferris 2000, 64-5.

march, and the frantic disorder and lawlessness of the retreating Dacians.[176] This contrast is a classic theme of "Roman versus other," which highlights and rationalizes the need for Roman rule in barbarian lands. James Packer notes that, "all the visible artistic symbols around the Area Fori commemorated this (Trajan's) military prowess".[177] Inscriptions within the Forum of Trajan note that it was financed, "ex manubiis" or from spoils, revealing that the conquered Dacians had financed the building of the forum and the column (Figure 27).[178] Packer agrees with Ferris that the column, and by extension the forum, was an architectural celebration of Trajan's success in war over the forces of disorder, chaos, and otherness that the Dacians represented.[179]

After his victory Trajan erected another monument, this one in the province of Moesia Inferior at Adamklissi (in present day Romania). It is an impressive circular stepped trophy monument made of earth and reveted in stone. It is 34 meters in diameter with 54 sculptured metopes around it, and sculptures of bound barbarian prisoners adorning the base.[180] Forty-nine metopes survive today, which depict similar scenes to those found on the Great Trajanic Frieze and Trajan's column. Roman soldiers fight one on one with Dacians, the Emperor is seen in *adlocutio* scenes, and Dacian civilians are depicted fleeing their territory.[181] This trophy was bold, not just for its colossal size, but for the fact that is erected in the same country that Trajan just defeated. In addition, Diana Kleiner notes that while the sculptural program here is similar to monuments in Rome erected by Trajan, this monument is provincial, artistically.[182] The craftsmanship is poor-

---

[176] Ibid., 66.
[177] Packer 1997, 282.
[178] Ibid.
[179] Ibid.
[180] Ferris 2000, 69.
[181] Kleiner 1002, 231.
[182] Ibid., 232.

er, and the proportions of the human body are roughly sketched and not anatomically correct (Figure 28). Made of locally sourced limestone and crafted by local artists, this monument is an example of provincial art, erected in honor of Mars Ultor, the patron god of the Roman army.[183] It seems that the Adamklissi monument was meant as an equivalent to the Column of Trajan in Rome, commemorating the Emperor's victory while also honoring the soldiers who fought in the campaigns.

Likewise, the Great Trajanic Frieze, which adorned a wall or podium at the north end of the Forum of Trajan in Rome was meant to emphasize the crushing defeat of the Dacians by Trajan. This frieze is thought to have been 30 meters long and 3 meters high, suggesting a grand canvas for the viewer to survey.[184] The subject is the same as on the column, which stood in close proximity to it, but Trajan himself plays a more prominent role in the frieze. While Trajan gives directions to his armies, surveys battles, and grants clemency to barbarians on the column, he is shown actively participating in battle on the frieze. This active participation signals his courage in battle and reinforces the overall message of Roman military order crushing the chaos of barbarian Dacia.[185] This depiction follows the pattern of the other Trajanic representations of Dacians as a proud but uncivilized people, who need to be subdued by Rome.

Latin authors do not provide much information about the Dacians, who are mentioned sparsely throughout Roman literature. In his *Histories*, Tacitus describes the Dacians as smartly opportunistic, though he notes that, "Dacorum gens numquam fida" or "the Dacians, a race never trustworthy".[186] The Dacians are not to be trusted, and crisis is

---

[183] Ibid.
[184] Ferris 2000, 74.
[185] Ibid., 75.
[186] Tacitus, *The Histories*, 3.46.2.

only averted by "fortuna populi Romani" or "the fortune (good luck) of the Roman people".[187] Likewise Juvenal, writing his satires in the early 100's CE and known for his dislike of foreigners, did not write ill of the Dacians, but instead seemed to see the rich men the Dacians encountered (including Trajan and a Praetorian Guard named Cornelius Fuscus) as the true root of evil, since they lived in frivolous excess.[188] This lack of feeling towards the Dacians, however, can most likely be attributed to Juvenal encountering very few of them rather than a benign attitude towards them. Zvi Yavetz notes that it is clear the Romans actively noticed and understood that they were different from other cultural and ethnic groups they encountered and they also actively attempted to belittle and dominate these groups. Roman superiority hinged on portraying outsiders as lawless and fierce, but not too fierce to avoid being subdued by the superior Romans. The Romans thought of Dacians as "noble savages" and their ultimate defeat was inevitable. This sort of world view allowed the Romans to see outsiders as barbarians, who could, with proper Roman guidance, be brought into the fold of civilization. This characterization is mirrored in the artistic representations sponsored by Trajan after the Dacian defeat, and rationalizes Roman cultural dominance over native cultures.

---

[187] Ibid.
[188] Juvenal, *Satire IV*, 111-112.

Chapter 4: Identity at Sarmizegetusa

Becoming Roman?

Identity is expressed in a multitude of ways, some of which are overt and others which are more subtle. A person can express multiple identities at a time, individual, social, religious, ethnic, and cultural. These identities can be marked on an individual level by clothing, hair, ornamentation, makeup, and body markers such as tattoos. They can also be marked on a larger scale, with identity expressed through house style and size, mode and means of transportation, and public declarations such as dedicatory monuments. Each type of identity can be challenging to recognize in the archaeological record. The methods we must rely on to study identity are deeply flawed and they require us to make assumptions about elements of the record that may or may not reflect a person's individual, social, or cultural identity. This paper is mainly concerned with how the relationship between Roman and native Dacian cultural identities were shaped in the Dacian province. As discussed in chapter 2, there are inherent difficulties associated with recognizing non-Roman identity in the context of a colonial system that naturally dominates the cultures it comes into contact with, whether by conscious erasure or subconscious modes of suppression. Nonetheless, modern scholars have agreed that emphasis of the bilateral nature of cultural exchange must be addressed even when dealing with a colonial system. This means that the agency of native populations can't be ignored when analyzing cultural identity. In chapter 2, I asserted that Greg Woolf's definition of Romanization would be followed in this paper, whereby native populations begin to think of themselves as Roman and work to create a new cultural identity that is no longer wholly native or Roman. I will now review the evidence at Sarmizegetusa to determine if these criteria have been met and if Romanization can be tangibly detected at the site.

To date, there seems to be no archaeological evidence for deliberate signs of rejection towards the process of Romanization in Dacia by the native population.[189] Evidence of rejection would include deliberate omission of Roman material culture, architectural styles, and association with Roman culture such as adherence to Roman religion. Otlean takes an "innocent until proven guilty" approach to Dacian rejection of Roman culture, though I would stress that a lack of evidence doesn't mean that this rejection didn't happen. The truth is often more complex than we would wish it to be, and I think it is plausible that a good deal of the Dacian population did reject Roman occupation and cultural transmission, as is depicted on a panel from the Adamklissi monument, where Dacians are shown gathering their belongings and fleeing the oncoming Roman army (Figure 29). Those who didn't flee the new province all together could still have resisted adoption of Roman culture in rural Dacian areas that had yet to be populated by Roman colonists. As Diaconescu's excavations of the early Roman buildings surrounding the forum show, the colonists of Sarmizegetusa began to arrive almost immediately after the conclusion of the second Dacian War, in 106-107 CE. The rapid expansion of the city from wood to stone and the defensive trenches that have been discovered around the main enclosure signify that Sarmizegetusa's early colonists might have been worried about the safety of the capital in such a new territory.

The idea of a peaceful acculturation soon after two devastating wars in which Trajan's troops razed the old capital, Sarmizegetusa Regia, to the ground is doubtful at best.

---

[189] Otlean 2007, 225.

The first Romans many Dacians would have encountered as colonists would have been ex-soldiers, the very same men who had fought against them only months before. I find this reading of the situation as overly optimistic and I contend that for the first several decades following the Wars, relations between the conquered and the conquerors would have been tenuous in most circumstances. This is reinforced by the overall nature of the first permanent Roman settlement in Dacia, Sarmizegetusa. The best evidence to support this theory is the epigraphic records from Sarmizegetusa. Most of the epigraphic evidence at Sarmizegetusa comes from funerary monuments and public inscriptions. They are recorded in the *Corpus Inscriptionum Graecarum Dacicarum*, the *Corpus Inscriptionum Latinarum*, the *Inscriptiile Daciei romane*, and the *Supplementum Epigraphicum Graecum*. The two most seminal studies on the population of Dacia are A. Paki and L. Mihailescu-Birliba, both of whom have attempted to analyze the epigraphic evidence for patterns of ethnic identity and have come to slightly differing conclusions. Paki attempted to classify the population, as understood from the epigraphic record, by means of ethnic and socio-political position.[190] In terms of ethnic origin, Paki took into account that Romans had been ethnically mixing for centuries and thus he only attempted to assign a person with a general area of provenance for their name. For socio-political structure, he used two classes of citizens: *honestiores* (the most honest/best) and *humiliores* (the lowest).[191] Paki concluded that Sarmizegetusa had early Latin-origin colonists that steadily grew to include several other areas of provenance from all over the Empire. He insists that the lack of Dacian origin names doesn't exclude them from being residents, simply that they are harder to identify. He notes that there are several uncommon names that

---

[190] Alicu and Paki 1995, 49.
[191] Ibid., 51.

could be natives and that there is some evidence of Dacians holding government positions at Sarmizegetusa once tensions "normalized" in the 3rd century CE.[192]

I agree that there could be sufficient epigraphic evidence for eventual ethnical socio-political mixing between Latins, non-Latin Roman citizens, and native Dacians in the city, but I find the arguments that insist native Dacians were at Sarmizegetusa in the early years after the Wars to be unsubstantiated. Paki himself notes that there are no inscriptions bearing undoubtedly native names until a select few were granted citizenship under Hadrian.[193] Again, lack of evidence doesn't mean there are no Dacians at Sarmizegetusa following the Wars, but I believe that the archaeological evidence discussed below also points to an absence of Dacians in the city that can't be easily explained away.

Mihailescu-Birliba's epigraphic study divided the population into the urban elites, the mining region inhabitants, the lower and middling classes, and the natives, though he never gives the exact number of inscriptions he studied. His study did not focus primarily on Sarmizegetusa, but encompassed all inscriptions found in Dacia. Mihailescu-Birliba critiqued Paki's method, noting several names which Paki seems to arbitrarily attribute to certain parts of the Empire even when that name is also popular elsewhere.[194] His own conclusions, thus, do not always match up with Paki's, and he is careful to take archaeological evidence into account along with the epigraphic evidence. He sees almost all the urban elites in Dacia as foreigners, that is, non-Dacians. The few names that might be Dacian-born he qualifies by reiterating that their origin is still doubtful. He agrees with

---

[192] Ibid., 83.
[193] Ibid., 83.
[194] Mihailescu-Birliba 2011, 6.

Paki that Latins were the predominant colonist group in the 2nd century CE, with greater inclusion of Illyrians, Celts, and Easterners in the 3rd century CE.[195]

In the mining regions, he sees a mainly Illyrian origin for the population of gold, iron, and salt miners, and he notes that the Illyrians are known for these activities.[196] The population of Romans in these mining regions seems to be most intense from Trajan to Marcus Aurelius. In terms of lower and middle class Romans in Dacia, Easterners, Greek-speakers, and Celts are all mentioned in the epigraphic evidence, while Latins and Celts are visible through *terra sigillata* type pottery identified to be from Italian and Gallic pottery workshops.[197] From 107 to 140, the pottery was mostly from La Graufesenque and Banassac, workshops located in the south of Gaul. Later in the second century and into the third, *terra sigillata* was mostly from the north-west of Gaul (Lavoye, Treves, Rheinzabern, and Westerndorf).[198] In addition, Celtic style ceramics were identified at Sarmizegetusa. The ceramic evidence, when studied in conjunction with the epigraphic evidence, shows that many of the middle and lower classes in Dacia were a mix of Eastern Greek-speakers, Celts, and Illyrians. Lastly, Mihailescu-Birliba addresses native Dacians in the epigraphic and archaeological evidence.

Essentially, there is no certain epigraphic evidence from Roman Dacia that can definitely be attributed to a native Dacian. Mihailescu-Birliba notes that several excavations of rural settlements and necropolises have found Roman and Dacian pottery in simi-

---

[195] Ibid., 11.
[196] Ibid., 13. The gold mining regions were Alburnus Maior-Ampelum, Baita ,Crisul Alb, Ruda-Brad, Corabia, and Baia de Aries. The iron mining regions was Ghelar-Teliuc, and the sites with extraction of salt were Ocna Muresului, Turda, Ocna Sibiului, and Ocnele Mari.
[197] Ibid., 28.
[198] Ibid.

lar domestic contexts and some Dacian style homes were attested.[199] It is certainly possible that these settlements were rural Dacian settlements where Dacians were using their own native pottery alongside traded Roman pottery. However, the amount of Dacian pottery in the urban setting of Sarmizegetusa is extremely small compared to these other settlements, so much so that it is rarely discussed in the literature.[200] The flow of exchange from Romans to Dacians seems to have been steady, but the influx of Dacian pottery in clearly Roman urban settings is not equivalent.

Another facet of the argument comes from the literary evidence for Dacians in Roman Dacia. The 4th century CE author Eutropius mentions in his *Breviarium Historiae Romanae* 8.6.2:

"...Traianus victa Dacia ex toto orbe Romano infinitas eo copias hominum transtulerat ad agros et urbes colendas. Dacia enim diuturno bello Decibali viris fureat exhausta."

"...Dacia having been defeated, Trajan brought over from the whole of the Roman world endless numbers of people to inhabit the fields and the cities. For Dacia had been exhausted of men during the long war with Decebalus."

The main contention against this claim is that Eutropius is a Latin author with a Latin agenda and bias. He is also writing about events that happened two centuries before him. The belief that Dacia was "exhausted of men" after the Wars with Trajan was one held by

---

[199] Ibid., 31. These "Dacian style houses" are referring to the local tradition of house building that preceded the Roman conquest. These houses could be either round of rectangular, with mostly timber superstructure. Once Romans colonize Dacia, identifying a Dacian house vs. a Roman house becomes extremely difficult, since Roman and Dacian pottery are sometimes found together in the same structure.
[200] Ibid., 31.

other ancient authors as well.[201] In fact, the idea that the Dacians were wiped out has endured to the present, and some have taken the paucity of epigraphic and archaeological evidence for Dacians after the conquest as proof of this "extermination".

I, however, agree with Dan Ruscu in his assessment that a total depopulation of Dacia as a result of the Dacian Wars is highly unlikely. It seems more likely, as Mihailescu-Birliba also attests, that there was already a low population of natives in Dacia before the Wars. This is seen in the archaeological record with scarce levels of pottery production even at the capital of the old kingdom, Sarmizegetusa Regia and the small number of Iron Age settlements that didn't revolve around a hillfort before the invasion.[202] Some objections could be raised to these examples. First, some have argued that Sarmizegetusa Regia was not just a large production center for the Dacians and that most pottery manufacture was a domestic- rather than state-regulated craft.[203] Secondly, the lack of Dacian Iron Age settlements could be seen as an error on the part of excavators, who have not identified these sites out of ignorance of their location or inability to quantify these sites due to a lack of central databases that accumulate the numerous excavations undertaken in Transylvania since the 18th century.[204] More evidence should be accumulated to test claims and to catalog site excavations throughout Transylvania. However, to assume that Dacia already had a lower population prior to the Dacian Wars would give a plausible explanation why the Romans thought native Dacians no longer

---

[201] Ruscu 2004, 76-7. Emperor Julian in the *Caesares* and Lucian of Samosata in the *Icaromenippos* both mention this "extermination" of the Dacians. Some scholars contend that they got this idea from Trajan himself in his *De Bello Dacico*, of which only one line now exists or Trajan's physician during the Wars, Statilius Crito's *Getica*.
[202] Mihailescu-Birliba 2011, 34.
[203] Negru 2003, 28.
[204] Otlean 2007, 7-8.

inhabited the province after it came under Roman rule, since this claim can only be thought of as an exaggeration.

Regardless, we do have evidence that Trajan brought over a large number of colonists to inhabit the province, as Eutropius describes. Diaconescu estimated that 750 to 1000 families were settled at Sarmizegetusa at the outset of the town after his team excavated an *insula* of the original timber city.[205] The original enclosure also grows and the suburban sprawl surrounding the city could be extended to 100 hectares based on aerial photographs that identify features of the landscape that are consistent with an *extra-muros* sprawl.[206] Several other major towns such as Apulum and Napoca were also of substantial size, hinting at a healthy and growing population of colonists.[207] We may not have Trajan's *De Bello Dacico* but we do have his column in Rome, on which he depicts Dacians leaving the area they once inhabited in retreat before the Roman army. This depiction could indeed be factual and many Dacians could have fled Roman rule in fear for their lives. In light of this evidence, I think it is reasonable to assume that the incoming population of Roman colonists could have either outnumbered the Dacian natives or have taken over the arable agricultural lands (including those that surround Sarmizegetusa) while the natives moved to the hinterland and inhabited areas less desired by their new Roman neighbors.

Such a reading of the evidence is contrary to some scholars who insist that though the Romans brutalized the Dacians by seizing their lands, destroying their hillforts (including Sarmizegetusa Regia), and marginalized them socially and politically in Roman

---

[205] Diaconescu 2004, 103.
[206] Otlean 2007, 165.
[207] Apulum, the second largest Roman city in Dacia, was located 70 km from Sarmizegetusa. Napoca is another major Roman city in the north of Dacia which became the capital of the province of Dacia Porolissensis after Dacia was reorganized under Hadrian.

society, the Romans and Dacians got along rather peacefully after tensions "normalized" with the Dacians Romanizing themselves gladly.[208] This interpretation reads like the old Romanization theory, where Rome is seen as an Empire whose exploitation of the lands and peoples she conquered fed the military machine that the Empire so relied upon. The goal was to exploit an area's natural resources (i.e., land, minerals, and people) and then "civilize" the inhabitants by systematic acculturation to Roman ways. This "Romanization" was bilateral, with Romans in this new area accepting local gods, customs, or material culture and natives in kind accepting Roman gods, customs, and material culture. This often created a blended cultural environment in the provinces that could spread to other parts of the Empire (e.g., in the worship of Isis, an Egyptian goddess, in Rome and Greece).

However, the epigraphic and archaeological evidence at Sarmizegetusa has not supported such an interpretation. There is little evidence of local gods being worshiped, negligible amounts of Dacian pottery or small finds were discovered, the overall city plan is wholly Roman with no inclusions of local architectural styles or techniques detected, and no Dacians have been positively identified on inscriptions from the site. All the evidence points towards a Roman city with little interaction with the native population. It is true that a lack of evidence doesn't mean a process didn't happen, but when several lines of evidence all come to the same conclusion, a pattern emerges. If Romanization hinges on the native populace assuming some Roman cultural identity and vice versa, this process is not seen at Sarmizegetusa.

The Big Picture

---

[208] Otlean 2007, 3.

The claim that there is little evidence for Romanization at Sarmizegetusa is a logical one if it can be assumed that relations between Romans and native Dacians after the Dacian Wars would not be characterized as friendly. The most obvious marker of Roman domination over the native population within the province would have been the city of Sarmizegetusa. Its quick growth into an impressive city of marble with an amphitheatre for Roman style entertainment and its many stone temples to various gods of the colonists would have been stark reminders that Rome was in Dacia to stay. It is no wonder that while more rural settlements might show evidence of Romans and Dacians living together or at least exchanging goods, the urban capital of Dacia bears a decidedly Roman character.

However, the evidence for Romanization within the rest of Dacia is still a matter of debate. As noted earlier, Dacian and Roman pottery has been identified in domestic settlements and necropolises in more rural parts of Dacia, and some Dacian pottery has been identified at garrison sites along the border of the province. This phenomenon also follows a logical path, since the *limes* of the province are farther from Roman production centers and trade with the local population was mutually beneficial and well documented.[209] Native agency is taken into account using this interpretation, since it acknowledges that cultural blending can be a conscious choice on the part of the Romans and the Dacians in this new environment. Where trade between Romans and Dacians is more beneficial, such as on the *limes* of the province, it can be seen more readily. In urban centers where Roman colonists are self-sufficient in their manufacture and Dacians may feel

---

[209] Ibid., 166.

more marginalized, very little cultural blending is apparent in the record. Romanization does not have to be black and white, a fully Romanized culture or a full rejection of Roman culture. In fact, it is almost always a shade of gray, since individual, social, and cultural identity are at play in this process. This process can also undergo slow change overtime that is difficult to measure, since it is undertaken by each individual person or group with a different pace and intensity. This is what makes quantifying identity so troubling, especially in the case of Dacia where there is little evidence available.

A New Perspective

One of the main reasons evidence in Dacia has been so difficult to acquire or rely on is because of the modern political environment that surrounded and interfered with Romanian archaeology through much of the 20th century. Post World War II, Romania became a communist country and Marxist theory was the accepted model for archaeological excavation.[210] This meant that certain sites were favored over others for funding and permission to dig, while others that didn't fit the communist theory of social class warfare were largely ignored. Similarly, scholarly findings also espoused the communist theory of a heroic struggle by the natives to overcome the imperialism of Rome. Thus modern political agendas projected themselves back onto history and archaeology. Twentieth century Romanian archaeology also found itself at the center of a nationalistic debate between Romanian and Austro-Hungarian politicians, which Otlean summarizes briefly.[211] On the one hand, the Romanians wished to prove through archaeological research that the

---

[210] Otlean 2007, 5.
[211] Ibid., 5-7.

native population was quickly Romanized and there was a strong "Dacian-Roman continuity", in order to promote the idea that modern Romanians had always lived in the territory of Romanian since the Roman conquest. On the other hand, the Hungarians wished to prove that Dacia had already been depopulated before the Wars and fully evacuated during Roman occupation. When the Romans withdrew in 271-5 CE, they claimed that Romania was devoid of inhabitants until Hungarians migrated to fill the void, therefore allowing Hungarian claims to be made on Romanian land.

One example of how this modern issue has affected scholarly research is documented in Mircea Musat and Ion Ardeleanu's *From Ancient Dacia to Modern Romania*. Even the title of the work expresses the strong nationalistic agenda of the authors. In the 1980's, Romanian scholars were locked in a bitter struggle with Hungarian scholars who contested that after the Romans withdrew from Dacia the land was left uninhabited, so that when Hungarian settlers migrated there centuries later they could claim some hegemony over Romanian lands.[212] This assertion was vehemently denied, with Musat and Ardeleanu stating, "The Daco-Roman population and then the Romanian people, never withdrew from their ancient home, nor did they ever emigrate or immigrate anywhere, but continued to live in village communities of their own on Dacia's territory; such communities are in themselves evidence of the uninterrupted continuity transmitted from the Geto-Dacians to the Daco-Romans and from the latter to the Romanians".[213] These arguments have created a body of literature written by archaeologists that are inherently biased, making decipherment of the many nuanced arguments challenging.

---

[212] Ibid., 6.
[213] Musat and Ardeleanu 1985, 75.

In the last twenty years a new perspective has emerged, one I prescribe to, which attempts to unpack the ancient and modern evidence to present a multi-faceted view that doesn't obscure data to satisfy a political agenda. It seems much more reasonable to expect that Romanization was a gradual process happening in degrees of both time and geography. As the Wars faded from memory, ethnic and social boundaries broke down, allowing a more diverse and mixed society to emerge. Likewise, Romanization happened where Romans and native Dacians were more likely to interact, in small communities or along the *limes* of the province. Inclusion of Sarmizegetusa, the major hub of Roman power within this bilateral process, could have happened later, as Dacians began to gain citizenship and social mobility. This suggestion seems counterintuitive, since cities are often thought of as melting pots of cultural exchange and diversity. In the case of Sarmizegetusa, however, I have outlined a scenario where a brand-new city built soon after two bloody wars could have acted as a microcosm of Roman cultural hegemony, where both Roman and native elements were resistant to the bilateral cultural exchange necessary for Romanization to be successful. Such an interpretation takes into account the epigraphic, archaeological, and literary evidence available and this more "middle of the road" approach doesn't exclude the possibility of Sarmizegetusa and Dacia overall participating more fully in the process of Romanization.

Chapter 5: Conclusions

A Changed Landscape

With the present state of research, several conclusions about identity and Romanization at Sarmizegetusa and in Dacia can be drawn. Firstly, the archaeological evidence at Sarmizegetusa, which includes ceramics, glass, metal objects, and architectural designs and techniques, points to a thoroughly Roman urban provincial center which relied very little on the culture of the native Dacians in its social fabric. There is scanty evidence for ethnically Dacian inhabitants in the city based on epigraphic evidence as well, suggesting that even as the 2nd century wore on, Dacians were slow to enter into the urban elite class. The ceramic reports from Dacia also suggest that little Dacian material culture was exchanged at Sarmizegetusa, whereas Roman and Dacian pottery is attested further north along the *limes* of the Empire (Figure 30). All of these conclusions are to be expected from a legionary veteran's colony established in the heart of the territory the legionaries fought to conquer.

That natives and Romans would be intermingling more on the borders of Dacia rather than in the urban centers is exactly opposite to what was seen in Gaul. In Gaul, Gallic elites were successfully integrated into Roman military and political life and Roman trade was already an important part of Gallic luxury trade. These factors allowed Romans cities in Gaul to be hubs of Roman and Gallic syncretism which resulted in a new provincial culture called Romano-Gallic. In Dacia however, the capital of the new province stood as the center of "civilization" and "Roman-ness", while rural settlements and Roman camps on the border retained contacts with native material culture, language, and religion. In addition, the violence inflicted upon the Dacian people during the Dacian Wars couldn't have fostered good-will towards Rome or her culture, perhaps leading to a conscious or unconscious decision to refuse Romanization. However, the lack of Dacians attested at Sarmizegetusa could have been a product of both natives and Romans failing to share in the bilateral acculturation so often seen in other Roman provinces. Romans might also have viewed the Dacians themselves negatively, and there may not have been the economic ties and relationships with the warrior elites that had allowed the Romans to successfully incorporate Gauls into their own urban framework.

Going Forward

Further research must be completed in Dacia in order to substantiate these claims. More complete catalogues of the archaeological finds at Sarmizegetusa could potentially clear up some of the ambiguities of the exact number of Dacian artifacts found at the site. Further excavations of *insulae* blocks within the city and homesteads associated with the city could reveal the lives of private individuals at Sarmizegetusa. Lastly, new excavations of more rural settlements from both before and after the Roman conquest should clarify Roman/native interactions in order to more fully study the degree of Romanization present in Dacia. It is clear that a disproportionate number of Roman sites (or those perceived as Roman) have been excavated, too often with little focus on the lives of the Dacians both before and after the Roman conquest. At some rural sites dated to the 2nd and 3rd centuries CE, Roman-style rectangular houses are found near Dacian-style sunken dwellings.[214] However, these sites are described as Roman and any cultural exchange between neighbors goes unmentioned. This sort of erasure of Dacian presence is not due to lack of evidence, but comes from excavators themselves who overlook markers of Dacian identity. Archaeologists must recognize this erasure and make further efforts to articulate the role Dacians played in their own country if a more complete understanding of the relationship between the Romans and Dacians is to be achieved.

---

[214] Ibarra 2014, 169.

Figures

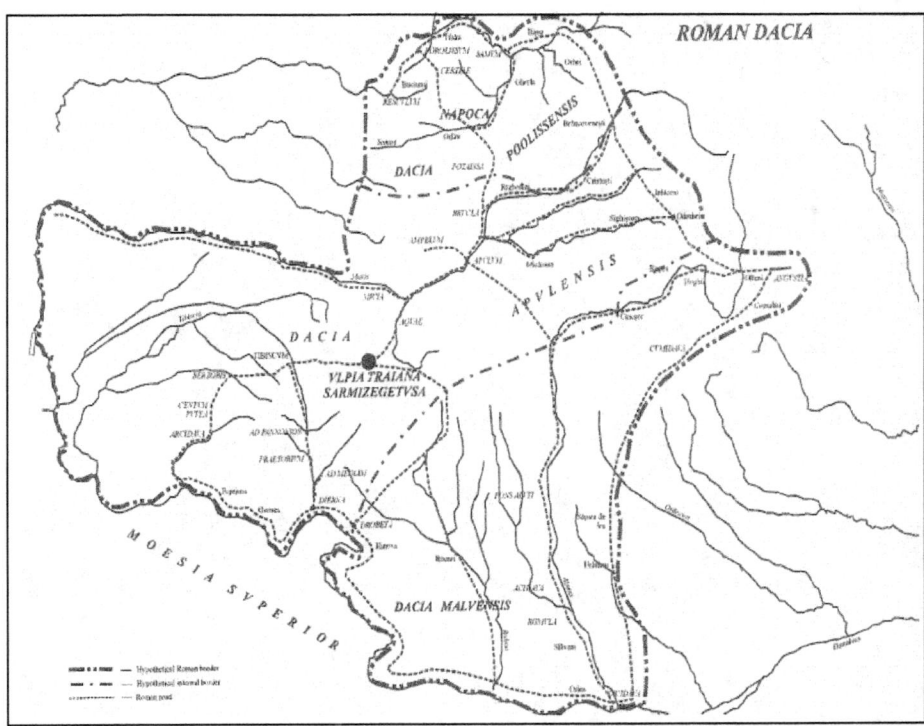

Figure 1. Map of Roman Dacia. In Gadzac and Cocis 2004, Fig. 1.

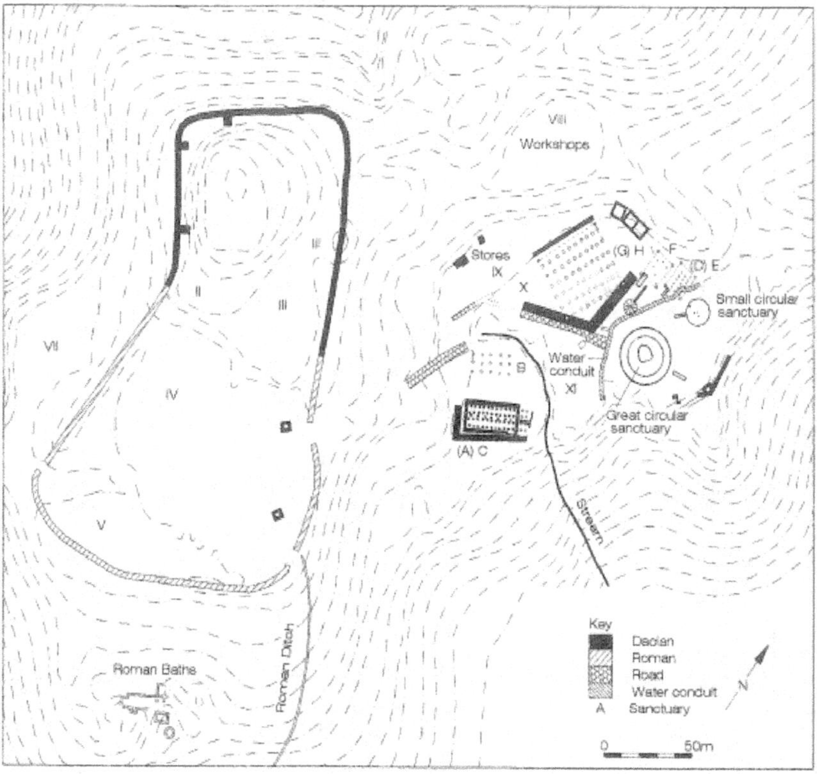

Figure 2. Map of Sarmizegetusa Regia. In Lockyear 2004, 43.

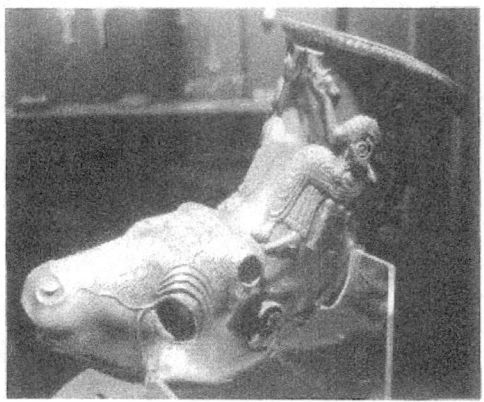

Figure 3. 3rd century BCE Dacian ram-head *rhyton*. In Ibarra 2014, 173.

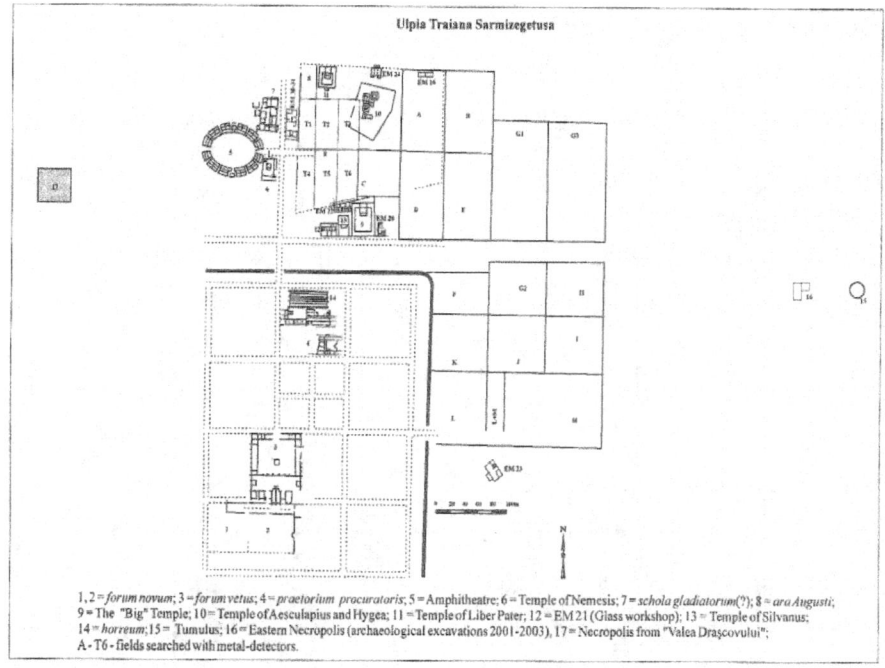

Figure 4. Map of Sarmizegetusa. In Gadzac and Cocis 2004, Fig. 2.

Figure 5. Dedicatory inscription of Ulpia Traiana Sarmizegetusa. In Piso 2006, 452.

Figure 6. Map of Sarmizegetusa, Late Antonine-Severan. In Diaconescu 2004, 104-5, Fig. 4.11.

    A. Walled Enclosure
    B. Trajanic *Forum*
    C. *Forum* B/*macellum*

    D. House of the Financial Procurator
    E. Amphitheatre
    F. *Area Sacra*

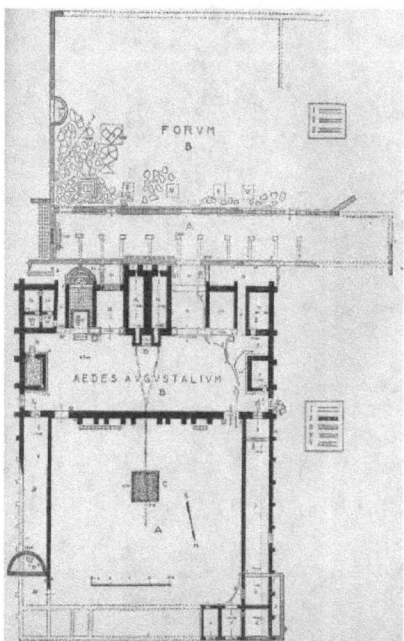

Figure 7. Plan of the Main *Forum* and *Forum* B. In Daicoviciu 1944, Fig. 3.

Figure 8. Coins from between 107 and 113 CE with images of Trajan's column. The first is topped with an owl, probably to acknowledge the placement of the column next to the libraries of Greek and Latin in Trajan's Forum and to impress upon the viewer the intellectual abilities of the Emperor. The second, issued later than the first, shows the column along with the base (covered in Dacian spoils) and the colossus of Trajan on the top. In Coarelli 2000, 11.

Figure 9. The base of Trajan's column with the entrance, inscription, and friezes of Dacian weapons. In Coarelli 2000, 23.

Figure 10. Decebalus suing for peace from Trajan at the end of the First Dacian War on Trajan's column. In Coarelli 2000, 132.

Figure 11. Trajan sacrificing after the completion of the Danubian bridge on Trajan's column. In Coarelli 2000, 162.

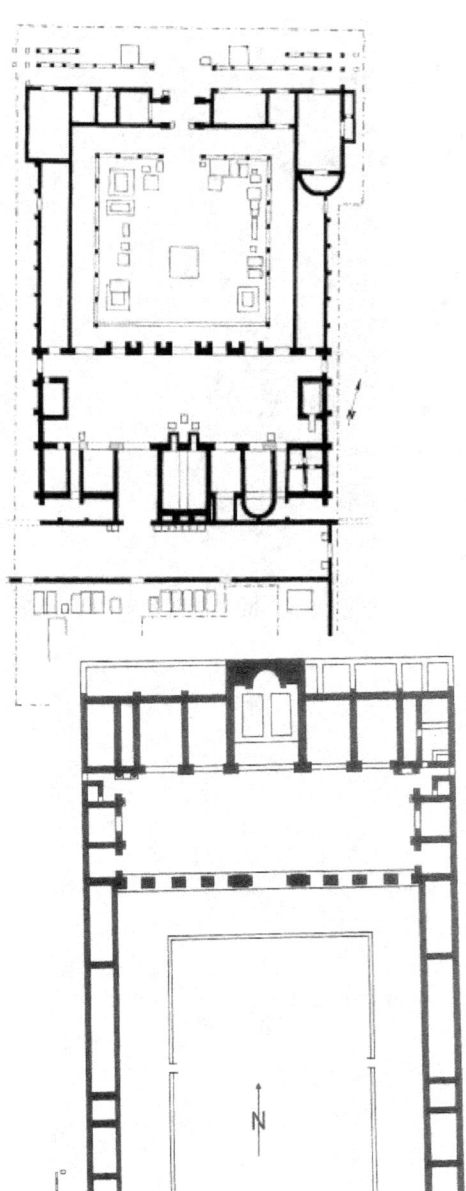

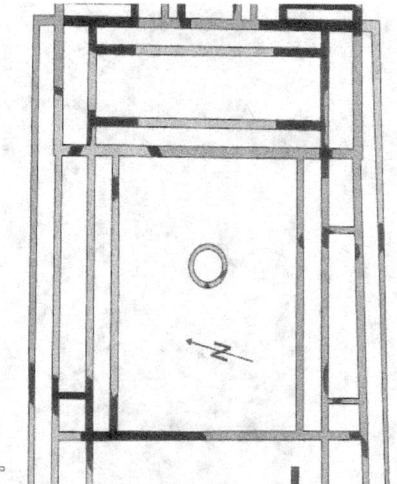

Figure 12. Plan of the *fora* of Burnum and Lopodunum next to a plan of the stone *forum* of Sarmizegetusa. In Diaconescu 2004, Fig. 4.3 and Piso 2006, 78-9.

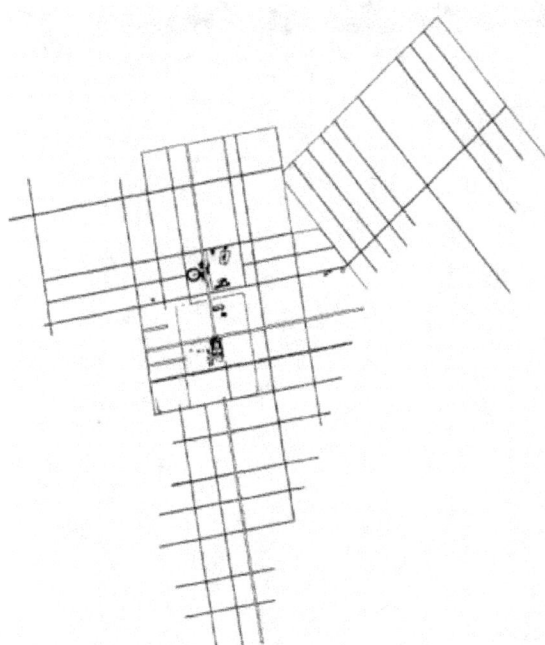

Figure 13. Drawing of the *centuriation* of Sarmizegetusa. In Marcu and Cupcea 2011, 549.

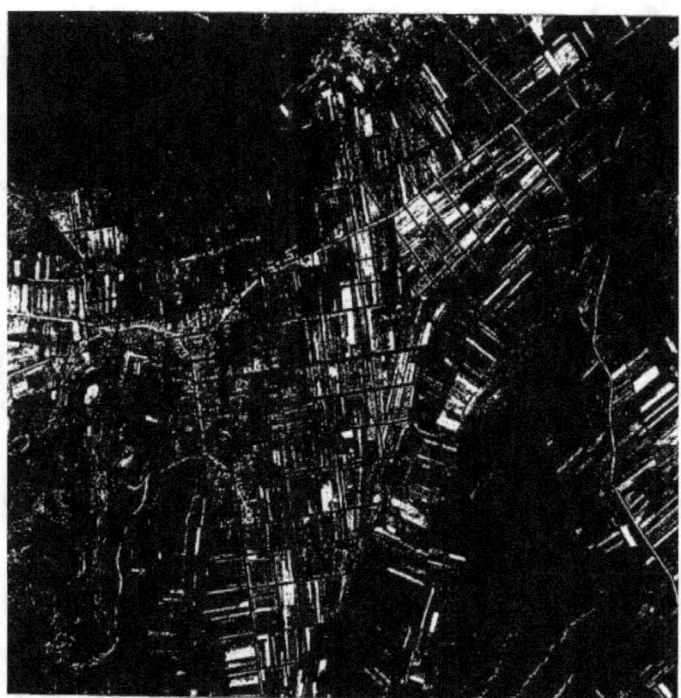

Figure 14. Orthophotos of *centuration* around Sarmizegetusa. In Marcu and Cupcea 2011, 548.

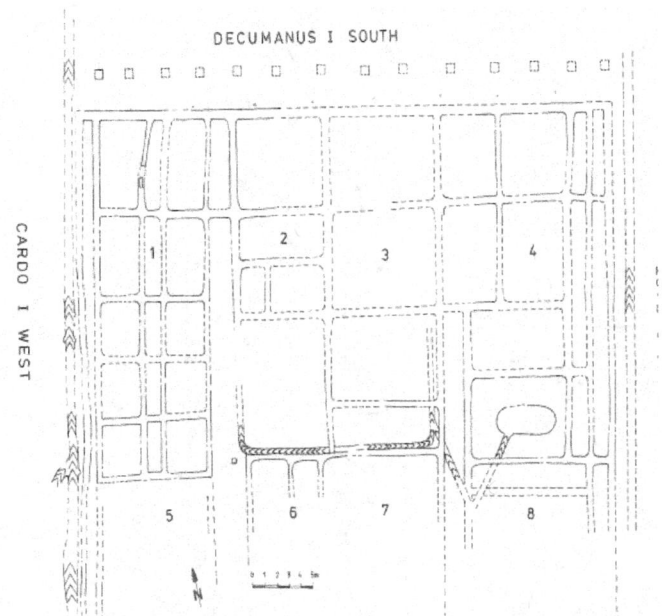

Figure 15. First phase of the first insulae south of the timber forum in Sarmizegetusa. Only the north half was excavated with 8 timber structures identified. In Diaconescu 2004, 98.

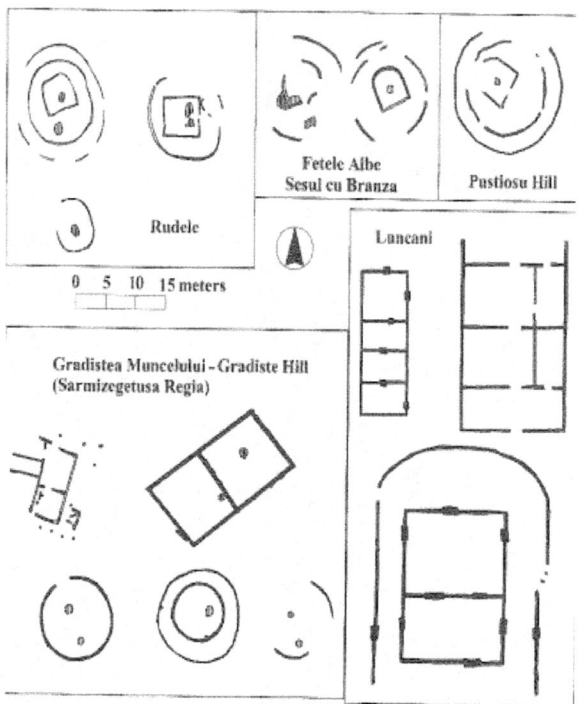

Figure 16. Different pre-Roman Dacian house plans from upland settlements. In Otlean 2007, 70.

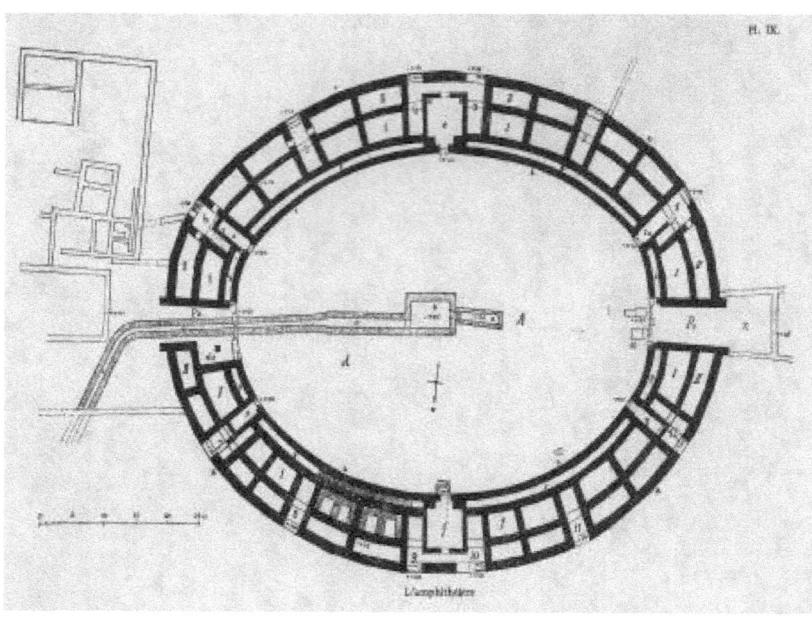

Figure 17. Plan of the first wooden amphitheatre at Samizegetusa. In Daicoviciu 1944, fig.9.

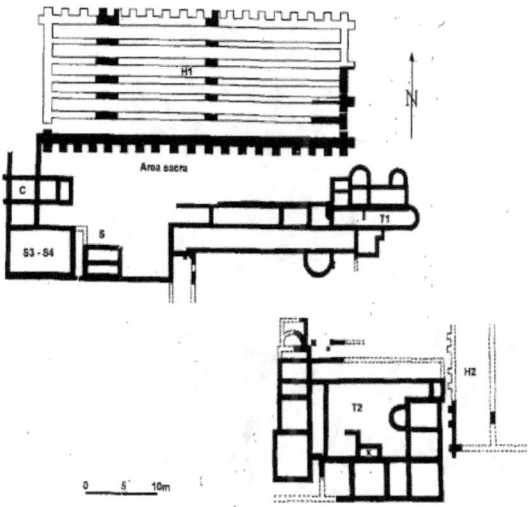

Figure 18. Plan of the financial procurator's complex with a *horreum* to the north. In Piso 2006, 454.

Figure 19. Aerial photograph of a stone quarry near Sarmizegetusa. In Otlean 2007, 184.

Figure 20. Standing column at Sarmizegetusa. In Alicu and Paki 1995, Plate LXV.

Figure 21. Statue signed by Claudius Saturnius. In Alicu et al. 1979, Plate LXVI.

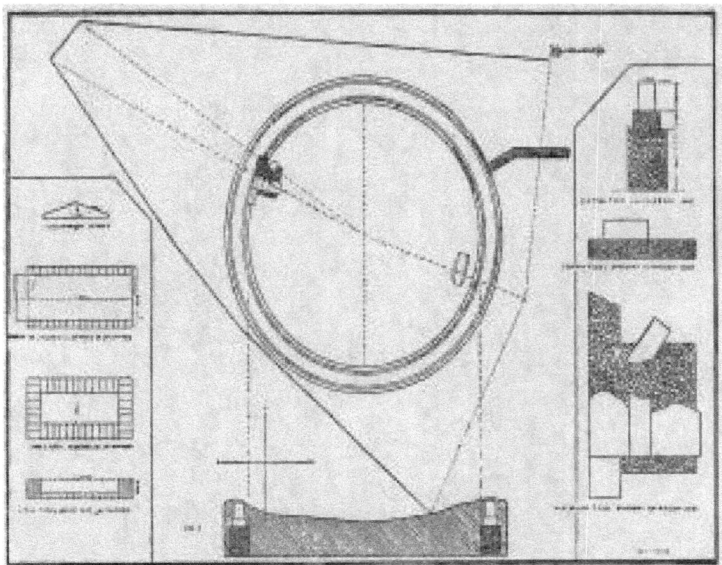
Figure 22. Plan of the Mausoleum of the Aurelii. In Daicoviciu 1944, fig.14.

Figure 23 and 24. Distributions of industry before and after the Roman conquest in Dacia. In Otlean 2007, 102 and 182.

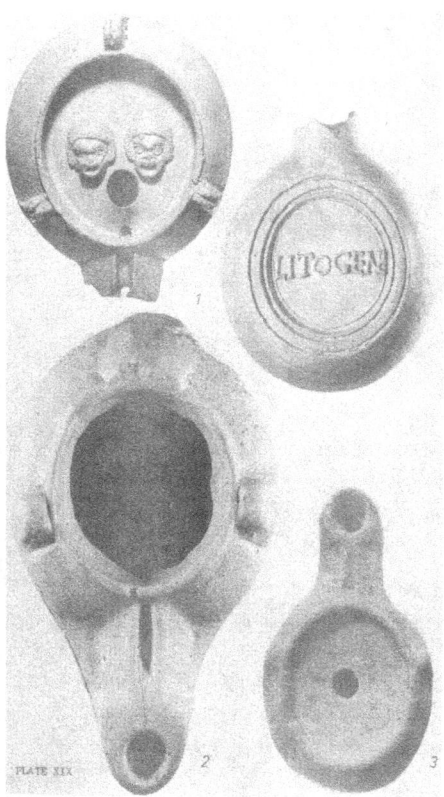

Figure 25. Roman lamps from Sarmizegtusa. In Alicu and Nemes 1977, Plate XIX.

Figure 26. Drawing of the original placement of the column. Note the Dacian weapons carved on the pedestal to indicate Dacia's subjugation. In Packer 1997, fig. 68.

Figure 27. Drawing of the original position of the "ex manubiis" inscriptions along with life-size Dacian captives above each column of the east and west colonnades in the Forum of Trajan. In Packer 1997, fig. 61.

99

Figure 28. Romans and Dacians fighting on the Adamklissi monument. In Kleiner 1992, 231.

Figure 29. Dacians fleeing the Romans on the Adamklissi monument. In Kleiner 1992, 232.

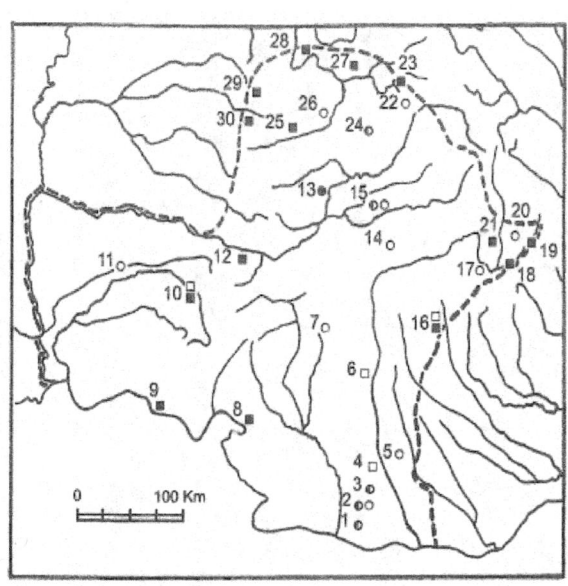

www.ingramcontent.com/pod-product-compliance
Lightning Source LLC
Chambersburg PA
CBHW050039080526
44586CB00014B/1366